Lakeland Birds

A Visitor's Handbook

by

W. R. Mitchell and R. W. Robson

*Oh! when I have hung
Above the raven's nest by knots of grass
and half-inch fissures in the slippery rock
But ill-sustained, and almost (so it seemed)
Suspended by the blast that blew amain,
Shouldering the naked crag . . . . . .*
                              Wordsworth

Dalesman Books
1974

The Dalesman Publishing Company Ltd.,
Clapham (via Lancaster), Yorkshire
First published 1974
© W. R. Mitchell and R. W. Robson, 1974

ISBN: 0 85206 226 5

Printed and bound in Great Britain by
FRETWELL & BRIAN LTD.
Silsden, Nr. Keighley, Yorkshire.

KINGFISHER WITH FOOD FOR ITS YOUNG

Lakeland Birds

THE RING OUZEL

75p

RIVER DERWENT, LOOKING TOWARDS SKIDDAW

Contents

and

Illustrations

THE HAWS, NEAR
MILLOM

The cover photograph, by W. R. Mitchell, is of an injured kestrel shortly before it was released after recuperation at a farm. W. R. Mitchell contributed the black-and-white photographs with the exception of the half title page, 4, 29 (Stan Lythe), 2 (Kenneth Scowen), 15 (Dick Hilton), 25 (F. Vear), 31 (Arthur Gilpin), 32, 49, 63 (Wm. Farnsworth), 47, 82, 86 (E. A. Janes), 51, 55 (Tom Parker), 84 (R. W. Robson). Map by E. Gower.

THE BIRD-WATCHER'S LAKE DISTRICT

An Introduction

LET us, in imagination, take the place of one of our Lake-land golden eagles which, having risen effortlessly in a thermal until it is simply a black dot under the clouds, takes in virtually the whole region at a glance.

We look down on the 866 square miles of fells, dales and lakes that compose the Lake District National Park, to which —rather than the Lake Counties as a whole—our book *Lakeland Birds* relates. The largest National Park in the country, established in 1951—and shared for years by the counties of Cumberland, Westmorland and Lancashire—it becomes, in 1974, part of a single local government unit called Cumbria.

The Park has a meandering border. It extends from Cald-beck, "back o' Skiddaw," to the estuaries flowing into Morecambe Bay; and from Ravenglass to the M6 crossing the eastern fells. Richly varied in landform, Lakeland is, in effect, one vast nature reserve.

Birds have no consciousness of man-made boundaries. We will not keep strictly to the Park and will include, for instance, a section on Leighton Moss, near Silverdale. Leighton has a special interest for bird-watchers, most of whom, approaching Lakeland from the south, can here initially and readily absorb some of the region's ornithological character.

Lakeland Birds (a companion of *Pennine Birds*) is not claimed to be an exhaustive work on the subject. Our book has been devised to assist the casual visitor to make the most of a visit. Specialist ornithologists can consult the published records of natural history societies, especially *The Birds of Lakeland* edited by E. Blezard, 1943; *Lakeland Ornithology,* E. Blezard, 1954; and *The Birds of the Lake Counties,* edited by R. Stokoe, 1962.

Scarcely any mention is made in this book of the teeming seabird life of the Cumbria coast, a subject dealt with adequately by another *Dalesman* publication, *A Naturalist's Lake District.*

If we could occupy the position of the high-soaring eagle, and looked down, we would notice first the mountains, which have been known to Cumbrians since Norse times as "fells". Many fells extend beyond the 2,000 feet contour. Four of them have summits at over 3,000 feet. Cumbria's highest point, Scafell Pike (3,210 feet), is also the highest point in England.

Names on the map hint at the old-time avifauna: Eagle Crag, Glead Howe ("Hill of the Kite"), Falcon Crag and innumerable Raven Crags. All the birds mentioned, except the kite, still nest here, though a red kite was seen near Wastwater in May, 1971.

Looking down, as an eagle, we should also behold valleys (called, again from the Old Norse, "dales"). They radiate like spokes from a hub, some of them being "dry" and others containing lakes that are edged by strips of good farm land. This type of land accounts for only about 2% of the total area.

The lakes range in size from Windermere, England's largest, almost 11 miles in length, to diminutive tarns that lap in the pockets of the fells. The elevation of most of the big lakes above sea level is from 200 to 300 feet, but Ullswater is about 500 feet and Haweswater—the former Mardale, flooded by Manchester—has an elevation of 700 feet. Of the small stretches of water, Red Tarn (Helvellyn) is at an impressive 2,400 feet.

The recent reappearance of the golden eagle as a nesting species, after an absence of nearly 200 years, was one of several highlights of modern Cumbrian ornithology. The dotterel, another rarity, adheres to several fells after years of persecution but the red-breasted merganser, which in 1885 "was essentially a marine species" that "rarely occurs inland," has spread considerably. The goosander extended its range to a lesser extent.

The greylag was re-established as a wild-nesting species after several centuries following the introduction of Scottish birds by way of a reserve by the Duddon estuary. Southern woodlands were colonised by the green woodpecker, where the peak of expansion appears to have passed, but the species is still extending its range, gradually working further north and, overall, slightly increasing in numbers.

Looking into the future, we confidently predict the consolidation of the collared dove (a rarity in Lakeland even as late as the early 1960s). The collared dove population exploded almost everywhere in 1973, with increases in nesting sites throughout Lakeland, particularly in the north. Here is a good example of how a new species can prosper in an already crowded environment.

Summering pairs of black-tailed godwit were observed for some years, such sightings hinting at the possibility that the species would nest, which it has done in the Lake Counties for a few seasons. Now a spread of godwits is awaited. The golden oriole, reported in Lakeland nearly every year in the

Lakeland's highest acres. The rock slope leads to the summit of Scafell Pike.

Grasmere and Keswick areas, has nested in Grizedale Forest. It may do so again. Increased sightings of the great grey shrike are probably a consequence of an increased number of watchers. This shrike appears in small numbers each winter and was seen near Penrith and Keswick in the winter of 1972-3.

We are concerned mainly with typical birds (Cumberland, noted Speed in 1611, is "overspread with a great variety of fowls") but rarities are irresistible. A Caspian tern swept over Windermere in the summer of 1959, and another appeared over

Leighton Moss in mid-August 1973. A snowy owl visited Tilberthwaite, near Coniston. There was a hoopoe in the Keswick area in the autumn of 1954. The bittern has been seen on fen-land beside Bassenthwaite Lake, but this skulking species long ago returned to the north-west and several pairs breed at Leighton Moss. A blue-winged teal visited Leighton Moss in early February, 1967.

Of the large, still relatively scarce fell-nesting birds, the peregrine falcon has begun a slow recovery of numbers on crags that have long been the English stronghold for the species. The year 1973 was very successful, due largely to protective measures taken by members of the R.S.P.B.

Ravens hung on in Lakeland despite a considerable increase in the number of walkers and climbers violating the traditional nesting crags of this and other species. The raven is now locally quite common. In more enlightened times, buzzards have re-established themselves in woodlands; the species can be seen regularly, especially in southern and western districts.

Some species have departed, or become rare. The corncrake was unable to adapt itself fully to dramatically changed agricultural conditions as, for instance, when the coming of machines and earlier haytimes caught it with eggs or new-hatched young.

Other species thrive as never before in new-style habitats. Conifer forests are accepted by many naturalists as worthwhile sanctuaries for wild life, whereas a few years ago they were being denounced as tracts of dreary monoculture. Coppice woods were clear-felled every 17 years or so and sustained a variety of woodland crafts; now (following the demise of the old industries), the woods have developed into mature, mainly deciduous woodland. The change has benefited wild birds, including green woodpeckers and pied flycatchers.

Increasing pressure by humans (to millions of whom Lakeland is now a short motor run from home) raises problems for those concerned with conservation. Tourism in Lakeland will continue and possibly increase. Birds are adaptable—up to a point—but too much pressure in any particular area is to be avoided. Meanwhile, a pair of lapwings nested on the circular reservation at each end of the Kendal by-pass in 1973. A pair of oystercatchers raised young between railway sleepers on a main line in West Cumberland.

Some Lakeland organisations are sensitive to the need to conserve. The National Trust, which was set up many years ago to preserve buildings of architectural importance or historic interest, is also aware of the need to preserve the natural beauty of the countryside. In Lakeland, the Trust protects 87,000 acres (about one-fifth of the area of the National Park). It has over 60 hill farms, and many of them are at the heads of the attractive valleys, such as Langdale, Borrowdale and Wasdale. The Forestry Commission, another major landowner, caters for wild life on its properties and, in recent years, has opened up its forests for public enjoyment.

The Nature Conservancy supervises a number of national nature reserves, mainly in the southern area. The Lake District Naturalists' Trust, formed in 1962, took practical steps towards the conservation of diverse wild plant and animal life by building up a series of reserves and persuading owners and users of land to conserve dwindling habitat types. The Trust also opposes development proposals that are considered harmful.

Manchester Corporation, which makes a large claim on the Lakeland rainfall by way of its reservoirs, has encouraged bird-life by tree-planting schemes, as around Thirlmere and Haweswater, and has also established nature trails.

*   *   *   *

The authors acknowledge the considerable help given by John Allen, Judith Atkinson, D. Campbell (Forestry Commission), J. Cooper, Leonard Cowcill, Jim Ellwood, E. Garbutt, Martin Godfrey, A. F. Gould, W. Grant (Forestry Commission), Norman Hammond (R.S.P.B.), Malcolm Hutcheson, J. G. Lingard (Lake District Naturalists' Trust), National Trust, Nature Conservancy, James Parkin, E. H. Shackleton, K. G. Spencer, John Voysey (Forestry Commission), G. L. Watson, John Wilson (R.S.P.B.).

AN IMMATURE LESSER BLACK-BACKED GULL

Basic Elements

WE cannot truly understand Lakeland ornithology without being aware of the nature of the rocks, the vegetation and climate to which the birds have adapted themselves.

Geology. Three major zones of visible rocks, lying in belts from ENE to WSW, are named the Skiddaw Slates, Borrowdale Volcanics and Silurian. None is as simple in its formation or its effect on the landscape as this brief statement may imply. Almost ringing the Lake District is Carboniferous Limestone and—seen outstandingly in the Eden Valley, at St. Bees and Holker—the New Red Sandstone.

Skiddaw Slates, of Ordovician age, the oldest visible rocks, are a mixture of generally dark strata—of grits, flags, shales and mudstones. They were deposited at the bottom of an ancient sea about 450 million years ago and are estimated to total a thickness of 6,000 feet.

Though termed Skiddaw Slates, these are not of the type that is easily cleft. They are, indeed, soft, eroding easily and evenly, hence the long, smooth, dark slope seen on such fells as Grisedale Pike, Mellbreak, Grasmoor and, classically, at Skiddaw and Blencathra near Keswick. An isolated but notably bold outcrop of the Slates occurs at Black Combe, above the Duddon, in the south-west of the region.

Hills composed of Skiddaw Slates have not the barren appearance of the next zone—that of the Borrowdale Volcanics. Here are fells that are steep, high-soaring, craggy and bleak. They consist of a mixture of lavas and ashes, accumulating to a thickness of from 8,000 to 12,000 feet. Compare the appearance of Volcanic country and that of the Skiddaw Slates at Honister Pass, where they are cheek-by-jowl. If you are motoring towards Buttermere, you see the former type on the left and the latter on the right.

The Volcanic Series was overlaid unconformably by Coniston Limestone, which is represented on the surface as a narrow band stretching south-westwards from Shap to Millom. It is

Borrowdale, which is a microcosm of Lakeland. Here are high fells, tarns, a lively river and "hanging" woods. The dale's name is also that for the region's volcanic zone.

composed of volcanic material and muddy limestones. The intruded igneous rock includes granite on Skiddaw, Shap and in Eskdale, and gabbros and associated rocks on Carrock Fell.

Silurian rocks, southwards from the volcanics, give a rolling appearance to the landscape. The distinctive crags and hollows are seen to the best effect around Windermere and Esthwaite Water. Silurian strata, formed of land-derived sediments settling in estuarial conditions, are made up of mudstones, grits, flagstones and shales.

The radial arrangement of the Lakeland valleys, or dales, extends from a central "hub" about High Rise. It is theorised that the infra-structure was superimposed when Lakeland had the appearance of a dome, the softer material from which has long since eroded. Flowing water incised courses into the older rocks. The run of the dales frequently has no relation to the rock structure.

The Ice Ages, the latest phase of which was at its maximum about 20,000 years ago (with a final melting only 10,000 years ago) considerably modified the Lakeland landscape. Glaciers of local origin deepened and widened the old river valleys, removing outjutting spurs, carrying away the screes and other debris, plucking out corries and scooping out some of the old river valleys like basins into which water, dammed by moraines, gathered to form the lakes we see today.

Boulder clay and solids brought down by erosion of the higher ground enable trees to thrive high up the sides of dales. Alluvium provided a basis for fertile fields at the dale bottoms on which farming greatly depends.

Vegetation. The fell tops are often very rocky and have a vegetation similar to that found in the sub-arctic because of the severe climate at higher altitudes. A restricted flora of higher plants is present with an abundant cover of mosses and lichens. Plants such as the mossy saxifrage are found only in the arctic and in mountains further south, but the majority of plants above the treeline are widespread elsewhere in moorland situations in Britain.

Vegetation on the fells has been greatly modified and impoverished since the last Ice Age, about 10,000 years ago, by man. Stone Age man cleared areas of forest, as did the Romans, but it was the Norse settlers that made the main impact, hence the abundance of placenames ending in "thwaite", which was the Norse word for a clearing in the forest.

A young hen capercaillie, photographed in Grizedale early in 1971 by Dick Hilton. This is believed to be the first photograph to be taken in England of a free-ranging capercaillie.

After trees were cleared, grazing by domestic animals often checked the natural regeneration of the forest. Sheep farming has been an important feature of Lakeland since the time of the monastic estates. The charcoal industry also affected the woodlands to a great extent causing the trees to be felled, in coppice cycles of about 17 years, for the production of charcoal needed to smelt the locally-mined iron ore.

Drier ridges on the Lakeland fells support grassland, with sheep's fescue as a valuable species, although changes in the patterns of grazing have led to the invasion of some pastures by mat-grass, an unpalatable plant. Bracken is also common, often spreading into pastures because of the less intensive husbandry practised on hill farms in recent times.

Heather is locally common, the most noteable tract of heathland remaining being on Skiddaw Forest. In marshy areas the flowering heads of cotton grass whiten the ground. Much peat consists of undecayed remains of cotton grass which still leads to the formation of peat under suitable conditions.

The highest-situated trees—a few rowans and birch—endure at about 1,900 feet, but the tree-line is generally at about 1,500 feet. High-lying oakwoods, relics of the old climax vegetation, are seen at Keskadale and Rigg Beck, in Newlands Valley, and Naddle above Haweswater. Quite extensive woodlands on the lower fells and dale sides contain native species such as oak, ash, birch and hazel. Alder, which borders many streams, is attractive to finches, particularly siskin and redpoll. The yew is a sturdy native. Lakeland placenames include Yewdale, Yew Crags, Yew Pike, Yew Tree Tarn.

A woodcock crouches on its ground nest in a coppice wood. The woodcock is a resident whose numbers are augmented by immigrants in autumn.

Conifers have been planted extensively since the 18th century, one species being brought to the district at an early date being European larch. Wordsworth looked at the new plantations, of quick-growing conifers, especially larch, and denounced the commercial enterprise as "vegetable manufactury." The "exotics" are now generally accepted and trees such as Lebanese cedar and Norway spruce no longer look strange at Tarn Hows.

Many fine deciduous woods in the southern dales are neglected coppice areas. Forests of conifers, overwhelmingly sitka spruce, have been planted by the Forestry Commission and have become a quiet haven for much bird life.

Some species, such as rhododendron, have been introduced as an estate ornament or as cover for game and have since run wild in many places.

Fen carr and bogs at low elevations are prime bird haunts. Bassenthwaite and Esthwaite Water have habitats of this type. Reeds grow by shallow lakes, such as Grasmere and Esthwaite Water, and in shallow bays beside the extensive Windermere.

Climate. A bird-watcher usefully relates his studies to the prevailing weather conditions. An example from 19th century Lakeland is that of a Kendalian, John Gough, who noted: "The cuckoo arrives in Westmorland about the end of April, when the mean temperature is 49° and the noon-tide heat frequently higher than 60°. This seems to indicate that a considerable degree of temperature is necessary to this bird, but I heard one crying merrily on the evening of the 23rd of May, 1814, when the thermometer stood at 41°: the hills were covered with snow and the wind blew strong from the north-east."

The Lakeland climate is varied but is generally wet and cloudy, as befits a mountainous area beside an ocean. Summers are not very hot, nor winters—apart from on the high fells—bitterly cold. The region is drier and sunnier than cynics like to imagine, though it depends where you go. Less than 1,000 hours of sunshine are annually recorded in the central fells area.

Lakeland's climate (more accurately, climates) has a number of sharp contrasts, such as between the floor of a dale and the top of a nearby fell, or between the western-facing mouth of the dale and the dalehead. In winter, many fell tops above 2,500 feet retain a Pleistocene chilliness.

The prevailing winds are westerly. Gusts of wind in Wasdale have been known to whisk water from the lake and deposit it on the Screes up to 200 feet. Yachtsmen on Windermere comment on the way the hills can break up an air flow so that in places gusts might reach them from several directions simultaneously. Another effect of this kind occurs occasionally on Honister Crag where the wind is divided by the fells into two main streams that are reunited with an awesome sound and savage effect. It is known as "the wind in the crack."

Lakeland rainfall totals decline from south-west to north-east. Felltops have a much higher rainfall than do the dales. On the coastal region, an annual fall of about 44 inches might be compared with the 150″ and 200″ recorded on fells less than 20 miles away. The well-named Sprinkling Tarn, beneath Great End, receives about 185″ a year.

Seathwaite, in a valley at the head of Borrowdale, is reputedly the wettest inhabited place in Lakeland.

Annual rainfall figures decline noticeably in various stretches of Borrowdale. Styhead, on the fells, has 170″ and Seathwaite (the wettest inhabited spot in England) 131″. Rosthwaite (lower down the valley) can expect just over 100″, and Grange (by the "Jaws" of Borrowdale) about 90″. Yet Keswick and Cockermouth (which though not far away are clear of the immediate effect of high ground) have 58″ and rather more than 40″ respectively. Coniston's annual rainfall is over 75″ and Kendal's 50″.

The wettest month in living memory was October, 1967. Over 24 inches of rain fell over a large area from Wasdale to Haweswater. In some recent years prolonged conditions of drought have caused concern.

Lakeland has no permanent snow cover. Snow lies on summits over 2,500 feet on about 100 days a year. The snow season on high ground may be extensive. The first falls can occur in September and the last in late May, even June.

The mean temperature at Keswick is 48 deg. F, but the temperature range on the south-west fells is less extreme than it is elsewhere. Areas near the larger lakes are generally milder than those lying a little way off.

Old Avifauna

THIS is not a work of history, yet notes on the old Lakeland avifauna—and, in particular on the way man has largely destroyed it—will interest anyone considering the present status of birds.

Ptarmigan nested on some felltops well within historic times. Pennant heard in 1776 that a few ptarmigan endured on the hills near Keswick. This fact was also noted by Dr. Heysham of Carlisle, in 1797, but these birds were probably mythical. An attempt to colonise the Skiddaw range with ptarmigan brought from the Scottish Highlands (an introduction recalled by one Jerry Smith, of Bassenthwaite) was abortive. Scots keepers reported "ptarmigan" on Shap fells about this time. Were they strays from Skiddaw?

Dalesmen, keen flockmasters, waged war against birds with hooked beaks. Raptors were thin in the air by the end of the 18th century. The survivors were ceaselessly harried by those who reared game for sport. A few centuries ago travellers in Lakeland commented on the survivors from the old avifauna: golden eagle, white-tailed eagle, harriers (hen, marsh and Montagu's), goshawk, kite, hobby, osprey, buzzards (common, rough-legged, and honey).

Confusion has existed in Lakeland between the golden eagle and its cousin the white-tailed eagle. A white-tailed pair were the last of the eagle tribe to lay eggs in our region until recent times. A pair of white-tailed eagles nested on Wallow Crag, near Haweswater, in 1787, assembling at the eyrie 35 fish, "besides 7 lambs and other provisions for the young ones." A pair was seen in Eskdale in the 1780s. (The species was, incidentally, last recorded in Lakeland over Coniston Water in March 1934). A bird was caught by a shepherd on Black Combe in 1838.

"Eagle Crags" are found among Lakeland names. Arthur Millard located a document, written between 1272 and 1307, relating to the Nichol Forest district of the northern part of

19

Cumberland; part of the forest was let "and they of the forest (the small tenants) must preserve the nests of sparrow hawks and eagles." This is one of the earliest references to eagles, which were common in mediaeval times but had disappeared as residents by 1800.

Historically, the golden eagle nested in Borrowdale, and Eagle Crag lies at the junction of the Langstrath and Greenup Valleys. Burtness Combe, in Buttermere, has an Eagle Crag. Other nesting places were Eskdale, Buck Crag in Martindale, Eagle Crag in Patterdale and Wallow Crag in the former Mardale. In 1677 eagles were reported nesting in Patterdale and Blea Crag, Grasmere. They sometimes nested near Keswick.

The last Borrowdale eagles nested in about 1765. Green, in his *New Guide* (1819), mentioned that John Vicars of Gatesgarth twice robbed the nest of its young. The Rev. W. Richardson noted that the golden eagle nested in Martindale in 1787 and 1789. "The first year the female was shot, and the male after an absence of about three weeks returned with another female. The next year, 1789, the male was killed after which the female disappeared."

Parish records of Crosthwaite (Keswick) show that over 30 eagles were killed between 1713 and 1765, the birds being counted as vermin, along with foxes, ravens and polecats. According to the Rev. H. A. Macpherson "a long and strong rope was kept in Borrowdale by subscription for the purpose of letting down men into the rocks to take the nests and young of Eagles . . . " The rope, which was also available for Buttermere, Langdale, Eskdale and other valleys, was in use nearly every year.

What price an eagle in the 18th century? The Crosthwaite records mention that in 1713 John Jackson received a shilling for slaying an old eagle and Edward Berket sixpence "for a young eagle."

The last golden eagle to be shot in Lakeland fell to the gun of Farmer Jenkinson, of Dunnerdale, about 1860. The late Ernest Blezard heard the story from descendants of the farmer. Jenkinson carried his muzzle-loader on his rounds, and had one or two unsuccessful shots at an eagle. He concealed himself, and ramming a "turrible gurt charge" of powder and lead down his weapon, he lay flat on his back in the heather. When the eagle passed over, he fired vertically, winged the bird and sustained a broken collar-bone from the violent recoil of a gun checked by the unyielding ground.

The eagle fell into a bobbin mill dam and "gave further account of itself before it was despatched and carried home to

Hole House Farm, where its full-spread wings were found almost to span the small kitchen."

For almost 200 years, the golden eagle was a rare vagrant. Then, in the 1950s, there were more frequent sightings. In 1957 an adult bird was seen flying near a Lakeland crag on which a newly-built nest was found. A three-year-old female eagle, found lying dead in Bretherdale, near Shap, in December, 1960, had one leg fastened in a rabbit trap, which it had possibly carried for miles.

The first golden eagle eggs to be laid on a Lakeland crag for about 160 years were two seen in an eyrie in March, 1969; the eggs failed to hatch, and the nesting site was forsaken for a new eyrie a little distance away, in 1971. Here a singleton was reared. This site, used in succeeding years, with moderate success, is wardened by the R.S.P.B. during the nesting season.

To a Cumbrian, the kite was "glad" or "glead." Clarke (1787) noted that it is "a native of this country and builds in trees." A pair of kites nesting in a tree near Ferry House, Windermere, was shot at the nest one moonlight night. William Pearson (1780-1856), who lived at Borderside in the Winster valley, noticed that the kite appears "on windy days in autumn." Pearson considered that the "glead" had disappeared from the Lake District, yet his old neighbour, Isaak Walker, remembered in his youth the pair that built yearly in "some lofty trees" near Ferry House. Ullswater area was one of the kite's strongholds; the species also bred near Derwentwater.

The last Lakeland kite was shot at Portinscale in 1840; another was shot near Carlisle, to the north, in 1873. Dixon Losh Thorpe acquired the stuffed bird at a sale at Threlkeld of property belonging to the Sawyer family. Ernest Blezard acquired the kite for the Tullie House collection at Carlisle and re-stuffed it 90 years after it had been slain. He found that the original operation, performed by a local craftsman, had been carried out with hay and something like red lead. The kite was partly mummified and, by all the results, should have disintegrated.

Harriers were scarce in Lakeland by 1830. Now hen harriers are increasing in number and have bred in central Lakeland as well as on the Northern Pennines. The buzzard was "pretty common" early in the 19th century. Many farmhouses had stuffed birds on show. Isaac Colebeck, of Gosforth, climbed Pillar Rock in 1827 and destroyed three nestlings. Pearson, writing about the year 1845, noted that he had not seen the species in the Winster valley for two or three years. About 12 nesting pairs were reported from Cumberland in 1885, and today there can be that number in one suitable valley.

Of the smaller birds, the dotterel—a rare thrush-sized wader —has for long been a nesting visitor to the high fells. It was greeted on its arrival by men who slew it for sport, and anglers used its feathers for "flies." Incoming dotterels were also considered worthy of being eaten; they were "fat and sweet-flavoured." Nethersole-Thompson's monograph on the dotterel (1973) estimated that, up to about 1860, from 50 to 75 pairs nested in England, mainly in Cumbria. Only a handful bred regularly by 1900 and from 1927 onwards dotterels have nested sporadically on the fells.

Captain Joseph Budworth, visiting Skiddaw late in the 18th century, "saw some eight dotterel on the summit that let us approach within eighty yards; and, if I had not thrown a stone at them, I daresay I might have come near enough to have threwn salt on their tails." Budworth added: "They suck their food from under the small stones under which they build their nests." Thomas Bewick commented: "The bird itself, when stripped of its plumage, sells for 4d, but its feathers at Keswick are always worth 6d."

An egg taken from a dotterel nest on Skiddaw came into the possession of Dr. John Heysham, of Carlisle, in 1785, and the reference to it he penned is the first-known description of an egg of this species. Thomas Coulthard Heysham, the doctor's son, continued the family interest in dotterels. In 1834, William Camm, of Keswick, sent him a hamper containing five dotterel, the accompanying note indicating that one bird was alive when the hamper was packed. Camm apologised because no dotterel eggs were available; yet some shepherds were looking for them.

John Cooper, another dotterel-seeker (sent by Thomas Heysham) walked from Carlisle to Hellvellyn, found the pair, but not the nest, slept on the fell, located the nest early next morning and walked back to Carlisle with the eggs. William Hewitson located a dotterel nest on Robinson.

Apart from local breeders, Cumbrian fells and coastline are traversed by small migratory groups of dotterels, known as *trips*. They are regular in their movements but far less common than they were.

A white raven, "bred in Cumberland," was seen in London by John Evelyn (1658). A headage payment for ravens was customary in Lakeland parishes. The Rev. J. Whiteside, in his book *Shappe in Bygone Days,* quotes that between 1718 and

1795 payment was 4d. a bird. In 1784, Clarke (*Survey of the Lakes*) wrote: "Ravens we have few, owing, I suppose, to the reward given for killing them."

A young Cumbrian raven in the early stages of acquiring its feathers.

When Wordsworth was a boy he saw bunches of unfledged ravens, on which rewards had been claimed, exhibited in Hawkshead churchyard. Hawkshead paid 4d for a raven until 1784. In 1782, at the age of 12, young William Wordsworth and Tom Usher, "Tailor Tyson" Fletcher, William Raincock of Rayrigg, and others, went to Yewdale Crags near Coniston to rob a raven's nest. Nearly 1,000 ravens were destroyed for reward in Greystoke parish between 1752 and 1842. In 1886 the raven was "local" in Cumberland, nesting in "about a dozen localities."

Incidentally, Wordsworth had an ornithologist's eye. He was by Ullswater on a November day in 1805 when he saw "a raven, not hovering like the kite, for that is not the habit of the bird; but passing onward with a straight-forward perseverance, and timing the motion of its wings to its own croaking. The waters were agitated; and the iron tone of the raven's voice, which strikes upon the ear at all times as the more dolorous from its regularity, was in fine keeping with the wild scene before our eyes."

Tree-nesting by ravens still occurs on the northern fells. Sandford (1675) explained that Crosby Ravensworth was so called "of the Ravens Timbring in the Timber Trees ther, but now not a timber Tree standing." Early in the 19th century tall trees in low-lying districts were frequently chosen for nesting, but most ravens now build on crag ledges.

*   *   *

The 19th century was a great period for bird classification, and innumerable specimens were needed. Mr. J. W. Harris, a member of an old Quaker family of Cockermouth, collected (between 1860 and 1870) one or more specimens of every bird then on the British List, which collection became the nucleus of that at Tullie House, Carlisle, opened in 1893, the year when a natural history society was formed in the city.

A section for natural history was developed by the Rev. Hugh Alexander Macpherson, author of *The Vertebrate Fauna of Lakeland,* 1892 (still the most valuable historical work on the region's bird life). Macpherson, who was appointed curate of St. Cuthbert's church, Carlisle, in 1882, became a zoologist of international repute. Another enthusiastic supporter at Carlisle was Dixon Losh Thorpe, who continued the museum work after Macpherson's day. Tullie House acquired a regional theme when Ernest Blezard took over in 1926.

The Rev. H. H. Symmonds, a keen conservationist, founded —and was the first secretary of—the Friends of the Lake District. Mr. Symmonds promoted a bird protection committee in the spring of 1939 mainly to protect the peregrine falcon. Sadly the wartime cull of peregrines in various parts of Britain nullified the work. Yet today there are many individuals and organisations carrying on the spirit of the work. The peregrine would not endure in Lakeland without such protection.

Entries in old *Transactions* reflect changes in the status of bird species and in the opinions about bird life held by Cumbrian naturalists. There is a record of a turnstone seen on Ullswater in 1801 by Dr. John Heysham; of a red-necked grebe shot on Windermere in 1912, and of pied flycatchers using nest-boxes erected as a pioneering scheme by Arthur Astley at Windermere in May, 1907.

The tree sparrow was first recorded for Westmorland at Troutbeck, Windermere, in 1907. A pair of nuthatches bred at Whitbarrow in 1916, a gannet was seen fishing Windermere in 1914 and a long-tailed duck and guillemot were seen on Windermere between 1919 and 1922.

It is through a host of such observations, spread over many years, that Lakeland ornithology acquired considerable historical depth.

Tree sparrow. The bird shown is a male, with food, at a nest hole in an apple tree.

Typical Nesting Birds

THIS section relates distinctive species of bird to the land-types in which they are most frequently seen.

The Fells "Fell" is unimproved land with a wide range of vegetation types: it is often common land—common, that is, to the local farms. Large areas of Lakeland remain unenclosed and unimproved.

The dotterel, rare nester on the Cumbrian hills, has usually been found at about 2,500 feet above sea level but now tends to nest at lower elevations. Another rare fell-nester, the golden eagle, chooses remote sites but collects most of its food in a lower countryside. Quite lengthy feeding flights may take place, so the visiting birdwatcher's chance of seeing the bird away from the eyrie is quite good. The golden eagle is most active at first-light.

The buzzard made a last stand, in the face of man's intolerance, on high and remote crags, but relaxation in keepering —and a more enlightened opinion about the role of raptors in the natural scheme—led to a shift by some Lakeland buzzards to tree-nesting in woodland. The food-hunting area is mainly rough ground between the open fells and woodland, and birds are seen in soaring flight over the fells on the springtime breezes.

Two pairs of buzzards, nesting near Windermere Youth Hostel in 1971, testified to the spread from high crags. A buzzard seldom lays before the end of April, and even then it may have to withstand falls of snow. The late Bentley Beetham photographed a nest on which only the cup, where the bird had been sitting, was clear of snow. The buzzard feeds on young birds and small mammals but also takes sheep carrion. Minor shifts in the areas frequented by buzzard occurred when myxomatosis destroyed large numbers of rabbits. For instance, myxomatosis swept through the Duddon Valley as recently as

August, 1972, and it was noted that the remaining four pairs of buzzards resorted to mice, voles, beetles, grass snakes, slow worms and adders, plus fish stranded by the river. Myxomatosis flares up periodically in most areas. Lakeland ornithologists have frequently noted the more catholic taste of buzzards in the near-absence of rabbits.

The peregrine falcon, a true crag-nester, has always been under pressure from man. Following breeding failures in the 1940s and a widespread population decline in the 1950s (mainly as a result of wartime culling and then a general onslaught against the peregrine by the pigeon-racing fraternity) adult birds were exposed to acute poisoning following the use of highly toxic insecticides, aldrin and dieldrin, as cereal seed-dressings. The peregrine, at the head of the food chain, was at particular risk. Since 1962 there has been a voluntary ban on spring-sown aldrin and dieldrin-treated seed. A gradual recovery of the peregrine population is reported. Modern threats are not so much from rock climbers (who in the main have been very co-operative) but the egg-collector, to a limited extent the falconer, and from the opposition of the enthusiasts for pigeon-racing.

Falcons normally fledge in early July, but some eyries have contained young as late as October. At least one Lakeland nest failed in 1972 when, in a period of most inclement weather, rainwater percolated through the nest, dragging and chilling the eyases. High on the list of food preferences of Lakeland peregrines at nesting time is the pigeon. In winter, some falcons remaining in the fell country move their quarters to more sheltered crags and others, especially young birds, migrate to the coast.

Lakeland, with about 60 nesting pairs of ravens, has a higher density of this species than equivalent areas in the Scottish Highlands. The flight call of a raven is commonly heard above the crags. Ravens have been holding their own in a changing world and the large population is sustained mainly by the corpses of sheep. The raven has been accused of killing sheep and lambs, but is dominantly a carrion eater. Many thousands of sheep are kept on the fells and at any given time there are newly-dead bodies to provide food. Up to a score of ravens have been seen at a fresh sheep corpse in summer.

In addition to the nesting population of ravens, a "floating" population of non-breeders adds to the bird-watching interest. Ravens attend communal roosts in winter. Ernest Blezard counted 60 birds at one roost; he also examined castings containing sheep wool and bones. The stomach of a Borrowdale raven was found to contain sheep wool, grass, bone fragments and 16 rough pieces of quartz.

Tree-nesting, as opposed to crag-nesting, by ravens has been reported from the Pennines for over 30 years. It occurs in Lakeland, yet most of the raven pairs nest on crags, an especially high nest being at an elevation of 2,000 feet. A typical nesting site is on a cornice fairly high up on a crag and protected by an overhang. The nest tends to be bulky and composed of quite large twigs of hawthorn, rowan and heather. It is invariably lined with sheep wool. A pair may make changes in the nesting site from year to year, or after a few years; but old sites are not usually forgotten, and in due course they are brought back into use again. A pair of ravens nesting near Windermere laid red eggs, which were taken by collectors. There has been persistent egg-collecting in this area.

Skylarks are locally common on open ground, but the commonest breeding bird of the fells is the meadow pipit which, incidentally, is the favourite food of the merlin and a favourite foster-parent chosen by the cuckoo. The meadow pipit nests on open ground where there is vegetational cover. Nests may be found on grassland overtopping some of the highest fells.

The ring ouzel, nesting bird on the fellsides, has been proved to overwinter in North Africa, the species returning to Lakeland in early March. It would appear from infrequent diurnal sightings that the arrival of migrants takes place at night. Some ring ouzels over-winter in Lakeland in mild spells. Most incoming birds go directly to their nesting areas.

The population of ring ouzels in Lakeland is not as high as on the best areas of the Pennines and few pairs are noted in the heart of Lakeland. Birds favour narrow rocky gills, also valleys with steep sides in which streams occur. Nests are found at around 1,500 feet, but with an upper limit of almost 2,000 feet. Shafts and levels in former mining areas are used for nesting. Ring ouzel nests containing eggs are seen from mid-April onwards.

Before the ring ouzel leaves for its wintering quarters, in early autumn, parties of birds up to 60 strong move along the fellsides and dine on the berries of rowan, thorn and juniper. Birds also feed on the fruit of the bilberry, a plant that is common on the ledges of many crags. Then the bird droppings have a deep purple hue.

Wheatear, another bird of "broken" ground, nests at even greater elevations than the ring ouzel, pairs having been seen at almost 3,000 feet. Wheatears also nest in drystone walls in the

Above: A cock ring ouzel feeding its young.
Below: The female standing beside the ground nest.

dales. The wheatear arrives at the end of March and disperses to winter quarters in late August and September.

The dipper has been found nesting at 2,250 feet (Stokoe, 1962), but this nesting site was about 450 feet above the average upper limit. Dippers do go higher than their nesting areas to feed. At lower elevations the undersides of the many single span bridges are favoured breeding sites.

The wren is ubiquitous; it is seen on high crags—even those above Honister and around the head of Wasdale—throughout the year, and is generally distributed on low ground.

A small colony of common terns became established near Devoke Water during 1967-8-9 but vanished completely in 1970 due, it is thought, to disturbance. Tern colonies are not unusual on the high hills and on mountainsides in Scotland, the Orkneys and Shetland. This was the first recorded instance of its kind in Lakeland.

Ubiquitous, and common, is the carrion crow. Nests are found most often on solitary trees, such as thorns, from about 900 feet to around 1,800 feet. The species is detested by farmers. It feeds on the afterbirth of ewes and, at the same time, will attack any weakly or ailing lambs. Crows roost communally in winter.

Jackdaws nest colonially on crags, and single pairs may be found nesting in the chimneys of deserted farmsteads or holes in outbuildings.

Birds seen on the summer hills include other corvines and black-headed gulls. They are feeding on hatches of insects. Swifts from Lakeland towns and villages take insects during racy flights over the peaks and plateaux.

Moorland This is a vague term. We use it to describe the rolling uplands from about 750 feet to 1,500 feet.

It is on such ground that a few pairs of golden plover may be encountered. Golden plover nest mainly in the north and east of the region, including on the wastes of Skiddaw, the Caldbeck, Armboth and Shap fells, but also on land above the dales of Esk and Duddon. (In contrast, a few pairs nest on the "moss" land of the Solway Plain). Dunlin, the plover's page, is less common. Preferred nesting areas are those with standing water, such as pools in peaty areas. The Pennines are the dunlin's northern stronghold.

The curlew is reasonably well distributed all around Lakeland proper and nests quite near the coast. Many pairs now nest in the dales, as opposed to high ground.

The merlin, like other raptors, was persecuted by game-

A hen merlin at its nest. The species is now quite scarce on Lakeland moors.

keepers and also infected by organochlorine residues, presumably derived from prey caught on farmland during its migration or wintering. It is now quite scarce.

Black grouse, which are found in much smaller numbers than formerly, occur above Grizedale, Kentmere, Haweswater, near Greystoke and also on the Solway Mosses. Blackcocks were seen *lekking* in the Rothay Valley in 1952. Red grouse are locally common, and Skiddaw Forest, which is still well-heathered, favours the species. Heathery tracts above Borrowdale and on Shap hold moderate populations.

Lapwings nest up to about 1,200 feet on Lakeland hills, using ground with gentle gradients. Redshank, found in the marshier areas, are more numerous in Lakeland than they were early this century.

Woodland   The highest-situated individual trees are rowan, thorn and holly. Of native woodland, oak and birch are locally common, sessile oakwood being the climax vegetation in the Lake District. Fine woods have developed from estate plantings in the 18th and 19th centuries. An early afforestation scheme with conifers was undertaken around Thirlmere by Manchester Corporation before the 1914-18 war, and birds now take advantage of woodland containing trees of various ages. At Thirlmere, native woodland was fenced off from sheep and has regenerated itself naturally.

Old oakwoods, with trees of various ages, extending in elevation to over 1,000 feet, are the nesting haunts of buzzard, chaffinch, willow warbler and blackbird. Such woods are usually deficient in shrub layer because of sheep grazing. Other breeding birds are the pied flycatcher, redstart and, locally, the tree pipit. The green woodpecker is moving into such areas. Bird life is naturally more varied and numerous where there are mixed species of trees with denser cover.

Lakeland's well-wooded dales (especially those in the south) contain many pairs of pied flycatchers and the population has

Cock pied flycatcher at the nesting hole. The species can be common in old deciduous woods.

risen where nesting box schemes have been introduced. Pied flycatchers prefer oak woodland. When nest boxes have been provided, the species has nested at over 1,200 feet.

A thin scattering of trees along a fellside attracts the tree pipit. Macpherson wrote of the species in 1892: "It straggles as far up our fells as trees or brushwood are found." His words still apply.

Given sufficiently dense cover, the hedge sparrow (dunnock) nests at high elevations. J. A. G. Barnes found this species to be one of the most common breeders in juniper scrub of the type extending up some fellsides to about 1,500 feet. The highest density of hedge sparrows is, however, at lower elevations.

The chaffinch can be seen in both summer and winter. Wintering flocks favour the mild south-west corner of Lakeland. Groups of about 300 birds have been noted. A lorry using the main Bootle-Millom road in February, 1970, ran into a chaffinch flock and 230 chaffinches were killed when they hit the bonnet and cab.

The most elusive finch is the hawfinch. The Rusland Valley is a good place to look for a species which is undoubtedly commoner than most people believe. The hawfinch also occurs in northern Lakeland. Listen for its distinctive call.

The woodpecker population fluctuates greatly. Green and great spotted woodpeckers are fairly well distributed. The lesser spotted woodpecker is considered to be quite rare as a breeder; it has a diminutive size, but draws attention to itself by being strikingly plumaged and vociferous.

The sparrow-hawk, now generally established where there is adequate tree cover, benefited from afforestation with conifers. Breeding areas include the Whitcham Valley, Ennerdale and the west side of Windermere. Hawks seen in one eastern valley hunt freely in varied areas—conifer forest, deciduous wood and open hillside. The plucking post of one Lakeland pair held the remains of redstart, wheatear, pigeon, ring ouzel and mistle thrush. A pair feeding young in a southern conifer plantation preyed extensively on juvenile starlings.

J. S. R. Chard has asserted that the new conifer forests provide a constantly changing series of habitats for wildlife and encourage a much richer flora and fauna than the hill sheep farms they are replacing. The most productive and widely used species are sitka spruce and Douglas fir. Other species to be seen are Scots pine, European larch and Norway spruce.

Grizedale, which is spread over nearly 12 square miles, is an outstanding example of a modern commercial forest where there is concern for wildlife. Here, apart from the extensive conifer plantations, is deciduous woodland at low levels. Birds have a variety of nesting opportunities.

Mallard nest in dense plantations as well as by the valley-streams. The "forest" ducks are frequently seen by Forestry Commission workers as the birds walk their offspring to the nearest water. Teal nest around the high acidic tarns, and nests are frequently in such good vegetational cover that the ducks approach them through tunnels formed of grasses. In winter, flighting duck at Grizedale consists of almost 50% of this species.

Grizedale was one of the areas chosen for the reintroduction of the greylag into Lakeland as a nesting species. An appreciable number of birds was raised here and given freedom. The feral stock found Esthwaite Water was more attractive. Today nesting pairs are sparse in Grizedale, though a pair of greylag nested on Wood Moss Tarn in 1972. (Greylag are, however, nesting generally and successfully in many areas of Lakeland).

The density of woodpigeons at Grizedale depends on the availability of food; a local numerical rise followed an improvement, through fertilisation, of the valley's permanent grassland. Clover is sought by the birds. From 1971 to 1973 there was a grand assault by woodpigeons on abundant acorn crops. Pigeons also feed on bilberries in autumn.

An "exotic" at Grizedale, the Reeves pheasant, was introduced by the Forestry Commission, in association with the Game Conservancy, in 1969. This was an experiment to assess how well the species would fare in a high-rainfall coniferous area.

Another "exotic" for northern England (to be found only at Grizedale) is the capercaillie. Birds from Scotland were introduced in the spring of 1968, eggs from the Central Highlands being conveyed 300 miles to Grizedale in boxes packed with hay, but none of the eggs hatched. In the following year, 12 eggs were collected and 10 chicks hatched, but they were kept in captivity too long and died. Fifty-six eggs were brought from Scotland in 1970 and 52 hatched. Forty chicks were reared and released.

A capercaillie's nest was found at the base of a pine in 1973, but the sitting bird did not bring off any young. Capercaillie are said to fare badly in the high-rainfall western areas of Britain, a notion which is yet to be locally tested. The capercaillie were introduced to Grizedale in years of lower-than-everage rainfall. Colonies of wood ants appear to be necessary to the welfare of young birds, and so colonies of ants were introduced to

Greylag geese, grazing. Grizedale, in High Furness, was one of the areas chosen for the reintroduction of the species into Lakeland as a nester.

Grizedale from a neighbouring area.

Thornthwaite, the oldest of the Lakeland national forests (it dates to immediately after the establishment of the Forestry Commission at the end of the 1914-18 war) is another dominantly coniferous area where there is good wildlife management. Planting began near summit of the 1,100 ft. Whinlatter Pass, a fact now commemorated by a cairn erected in Brow's Wood to mark the jubilee of the Forestry Commission in 1969. Some of the original trees have reached heights of between 70 and 80 feet in 50 years' growth.

The forest, which extends right across Whinlatter, continues round Bassenthwaite Lake in a series of detached blocks to The Dodd, below Skiddaw. The total area is 6,500 acres (over 10 square miles) but this includes 1,000 acres which are too high lying and poor for satisfactory growth. The plantations rise from lake level to nearly 1,700 feet.

Upper Dales   House sparrows are seen around farm buildings and at houses scattered around the upper dales. Tree sparrows occur in small colonies. The reed bunting can be seen in small numbers in more marshy terrain. Pied wagtails can be quite common in some years, a favourite nesting site being the dry-stone walls.

Swallows and house martins depend on buildings, which in the dales are mainly farm buildings. Small colonies of swifts nest in the larger villages.

Barn owls, typically birds of open country, are less common than they were. One pair in the Whitcham valley regularly nests on a ledge at one corner of a disused stone-built hog-house. The opposite corner is invariably occupied by a kestrel pair.

Lakes and Streams. The term lake, applying to a large stretch of water, is modern. Lakeland maps feature the terms "mere" and "water". Streams are known locally as becks.

Presumably, after the Ice Ages all the lakes were in very much the same condition. They have been changing ever since, some more rapidly than others. Wastwater and Ennerdale, the two least changed lakes, are virtually barren. The most changed lake, Esthwaite Water, lies a little way from the fells, in a flatter country that has been well-farmed. Nearly half its drainage area is cultivated, as opposed to only about five per cent of the drainage area of Wastwater and Ennerdale.

Urban water authorities have created reservoirs. Manchester Corporation flooded the former Mardale and also the neighbouring Wet Sleddale; the reservoirs are now inter-related. Manchester Waterworks Committee has claimed part of the overspill of Ullswater and Windermere, but has not interfered with the natural levels of the lakes.

The dipper, already mentioned as a fell-haunting bird, frequents Lakeland becks and larger watercourses that flow fast and clear. The highest density of dippers is in the peripheral areas of the Lake District. Hill birds may nest later than those

Coniston Water, where the red-breasted merganser is quite common. Greylags also nest by the lake.

on the lower reaches. The first eggs are laid before the end of March. Two unusual nesting places reported from Lakeland were the side of a tree (1972) and the top of a boulder at the centre of a river (1973), the latter nest being washed away a week after its completion.

Grey wagtail, a bird of clear, fast-flowing streams, is most commonly found where watercourses are broader and their banks are lined by trees. Most grey wagtails leave Lakeland after the nesting season, but a few winter on the lower reaches of the main rivers. Concentrations of yellow wagtails are found, there being one near Bassenthwaite Lake.

Common sandpipers nest beside lakes, tarns and streams up to about 1,500 feet. Holidaymakers, attracted to the same shorelines, undoubtedly disturb many pairs, but such intrusion has not been disastrous to the species. The kingfisher, which is not often encountered above 1,000 feet, became scarce after the 1963 winter; it has since recovered its numbers to become relatively common in suitable localities. (The kingfisher now nests successfully within the city of Carlisle).

Colonies of sandmartins are established in banks where the rivers broaden before entering a lake; sandpits are also colonised. The sandmartin's method of taking insects when on the wing has lured at least one bird to take the artificial fly cast by a fisherman.

The great-crested grebe nests on a number of smaller lakes and some suitable tarns. Shallow, reed-edged Esthwaite Water is ideal for the species which is, however, less numerous here than it was 10 years ago. In the northern area, this grebe nests on Bassenthwaite Lake and Overwater.

Since the 1950s, the red-breasted merganser has spread from coastal areas (it was once found nesting only in dunes near Ravenglass) to nest by lakes. Among the nesting areas are Derwentwater, Bassenthwaite Lake, Overwater and Measand Beck, (Windermere). The goosander has been added to the list of breeding species and a pair on Haweswater (1971) had a brood of 10 that was unfortunately reduced to three by predation. That year a goosander was seen with nine young on Ullswater on May 20. Goosanders have been recorded on Wet Sleddale reservoir, at Angle Tarn and Brotherswater.

Mallard are widely distributed and breed near many high-level tarns. The teal is a regular but fairly local breeder, and nests have been found on the slopes of Silver Howe above Ullswater. The tufted duck, a common species in winter, is represented as a breeder by a few pairs. A nest was found at High Dam, Finsthwaite, in 1967.

Cormorants can be seen on many lakes, but move in numbers during the autumn. Almost all the lakes and tarns have their quota of cormorants in winter with the exception of Ennerdale, which must lack sufficient fish as food, and tree-roosting parties of cormorants are observed by Windermere and Coniston Water. Cormorants have been observed flying over High Street in the evening and dropping down to roost in trees at the southern end of Haweswater.

Observations at Haweswater, in the period from March to July, 1971, showed that birds varied the places used for relaxing after large meals. The first was in an area of larches on a peninsula, and the birds were later seen perched on islets and dry walls. Early in the period of observation, birds of different ages were noted, but later in the season the cormorants present were seen to be immatures. Bassenthwaite Lake has several well-used perches, as also have Thirlmere and Crummock Water.

The greylag's return to England as a nesting species began with a rearing scheme at The Hawes reserve near Millom. The eggs of greylags of Scottish origin were hatched out here in 1961 and successive years. Three pairs of greylags nested in the wild at Coniston Water in 1963. Greylags are now breeding on many lakes, tarns—even garden ponds. At least three established colonies exist in the northern lakes area, with a combined total in excess of 200 birds. A similar number of birds is found in the southern area. On the western side of Lakeland the largest colony is normally composed of around 30 nesting pairs. Up to 150 greylags have been counted while grazing on private salt marshes, and up to 80 birds have been present on Esthwaite Water. A breeding nucleus of greylags is being formed in Ennerdale.

Greylag gosling, just beginning to feather. Lakeland's population of greylags has now reached about 400.

Some Bird Haunts

I N an area with a radial arrangement of hill ranges and dales, it is judged most convenient to arrange the recommended birdwatching areas in alphabetical order. The lengths and breadths of the lakes given are approximate.

Ambleside. A nature trail organised by the Ambleside Field Society and the National Trust leads through Skelghyll Wood. A leaflet is available. The trail can be walked in about an hour. Birds to be seen include jay, buzzard, carrion crow, woodcock, tree-creeper, goldcrest, warblers. Visit the National Park Centre at Brockhole, between Ambleside and Windermere, and also Bridge House, the Ambleside information centre of the Trust. An environmental walk taking in the Rothay Valley and Loughrigg has been arranged by the Charlotte Mason College of Education and the National Trust; the walk can be completed in about two and a half hours, beginning and ending at Ambleside's Bridge House. A descriptive leaflet has been published.

Arnside Knott (521 feet), by the Kent estuary and Morecambe Bay. A nature trail, arranged by the National Trust and local parish council, begins at the mountain indicator. A leaflet is available. Among the nesting birds are wren, robin, tit family, goldcrest, tree-creeper, bullfinch, chiffchaff, willow warbler and blackcap. The meadow pipit and yellow hammer frequent open areas, and wooded areas hold green and great spotted woodpeckers, tawny owl, jay, woodcock and nightjar. The Lake District Naturalists' Trust instituted a nest box scheme.

Bassenthwaite (4 miles long, 1 mile wide). This lake with a surface area of about 1,300 acres, and a mean depth of 70 feet, lies to the north of Keswick. At the southern end is the most extensive fen in Lakeland. Good bird-watching can be had at all times of the year from a lay-by near Ouse Bridge (north end of the lake).

In the summer may be seen chiffchaff, willow warbler, wren, robin, five species of the tit family, tree-creeper, goldcrest, buzzard, sparrow-hawk and, sometimes, the golden eagle. Wintering birds include large flocks of duck, coot, mallard, some teal, goldeneye, pochard, red-breasted merganser, goosander, great-crested and little grebes with (in hard weather) black-throated diver. Cormorants are often present. A large roost of black-headed and common gulls is another winter feature. Areas around Bassenthwaite can be satisfactorily bird-watched from a car.

Blelham Tarn (and 5 acre Blelham Bog). The tarn is situated just north-west of Windermere lake. Blelham Bog, a national nature reserve, is an almost unique example of a sphagnum bog developing from wet willow woodland. The tarn is good for wildfowl at any time of the year.

Borrowdale. This area, south of Keswick, is a microcosm of Lakeland. Here are high fells, tarns and "hanging" woods. Borrowdale leads down to Derwentwater, which is a bird-rich lake. At the dalehead, around Seathwaite, are (among many species) raven, yellow and grey wagtail, snipe and dipper. The carrion crow is common. Fine old deciduous woods on the fellsides contain pied flycatcher, green and great spotted wood-

Woodland in the Seathwaite valley, at the head of Borrowdale. Woodpeckers and redstarts nest here.

peckers, redstart and woodcock. A one and a half hour's walk arranged by the National Trust and the Lake District Naturalists' Trust extends up the open fell to High Doat (1,050 feet) descending through Johnny Wood. The walk begins and ends at Seatoller car park, and a leaflet is available.

Buttermere, Crummock Water, Loweswater. Buttermere (1¼ by ½) and Crummock Water (3½ by 1) illustrate the complete development of the division of one lake by the delta from a tributary stream. Loweswater (1¼ by ½) completes the trio in this attractive valley. Dominating the area are some of the shapeliest fells—Mellbreak, Grasmoor, Red Pike, High Stile. To be seen at the lakes are greylag, kingfisher, heron and sandpiper. There are sometimes wintering whooper swans and rafts of pochard.

Coniston Water (5½ by 1). This popular lake has, on its eastern shore, considerable plantations of the Forestry Commission extending over the hill to Grizedale. Red-breasted merganser are locally quite common; greylags nest by the lake and buzzards nest in local woods. Wintering wildfowl include goldeneye and tufted duck, with occasional quite large rafts of pochard. Fir Island holds a small winter roost of cormorants, a species which visits the lake to feed. For details of the Brantwood Nature Trail, apply to the Warden at Brantwood, Coniston.

Crummock Water See Buttermere.

Derwentwater (3 by 1¼). The lake, just south of Keswick, has a mean depth of 70 feet. This is about the same as that of Bassenthwaite Lake, with which it was united until infilling material from a stream divided one lake into two. The Friars Crag Nature Walk, of about 2 miles, was organised by the National Trust and the Lake District Naturalists' Trust. By Derwentwater, a visitor in winter should see mallard, coot, black-headed gull, pochard, tufted duck, goldeneye, heron. Red-breasted mergansers are becoming established. Cormorants come here to fish. Woodland birds include the great spotted woodpecker, yellow hammer, chaffinch and wren. Woodpigeons converge on Cockshott Wood in late autumn for acorns and beech mast.

Drigg Dunes and Gullery (583 acres). Situated near Ravenglass, the sand dunes were declared a local nature reserve by the Cumberland County Council and the reserve contains an important black-headed gullery and a ternery (common, arctic, little tern). Both flourish under strict protection. The estimated number of pairs of black-headed gulls in 1969 was 10,000. Oystercatcher and ringed plover are locally common. Permits from: County Land Agent, 1 Alfred Street North, Carlisle.

Duddon Valley and Dunnerdale. A well-wooded valley leading up to a dalehead and the new coniferous plantations of the Forestry Commission. Over 50 species of bird have bred in Dunnerdale Forest, the list including great and lesser spotted woodpeckers, turtle dove, sparrow-hawk, long and short-eared owls, goldfinch, kestrel, barn owl, redstart, pied and spotted flycatchers, jay, yellow hammer, buzzard, wood warbler, tree pipit.

Additional species breeding in the area as a whole include raven, whinchat and stonechat, golden plover, sedge and grasshopper warblers, greylag, ring ouzel, curlew, merlin, nightjar, heron, kingfisher, yellow and grey wagtails, partridge and black grouse. Wintering birds that may be seen are the brambling, whooper swan, twite. Species entering the area for feeding and roosting are black-headed, herring, common and lesser black-backed gulls, cormorant, oystercatcher, red-breasted merganser.

The valley has a notable population of owls. The tawny owl, the most numerous, can be seen throughout the wooded areas. The barn owl has colonised old buildings, even small quarries.

Ennerdale Water ($2\frac{1}{2}$ by 1). The lake (148 feet maximum depth) has comparatively little food for birds. The Forestry Commission's extensive holdings have increased the local bird population. There is also some semi-natural deciduous woodland. A list of species seen in the area during the past three years includes: great and lesser black-backed gulls, black and red grouse, bullfinch, reed bunting, buzzard, stonechat, woodcock, cormorant, curlew, dipper, teal, tufted duck, goldeneye, red-breasted merganser, goosander, greylag, raven, sparrowhawk, barn and short-eared owls, peregrine falcon, Canada goose, common gull, jay, the tit family, pochard, wheatear, green woodpecker, redstart, ringed plover, dunlin, grey wagtail, yellow hammer.

Elterwater. Near the village of the same name, between Ambleside and Great Langdale. Elterwater is little more than a series of reed-edged pools. The name is said to come from the Old Norse, meaning "lake of the wild swans." Whooper swans of Icelandic origin are among the wintering waterfowl.

Esthwaite Water ($1\frac{1}{2}$ by $\frac{1}{2}$). Situated near Hawkshead, this shallow and rich lake has had national nature reserve status since 1955. In the reed swamp and carr, at the north end, nest great-crested and little grebes, also greylag.

Grasmere (1 by $\frac{1}{2}$) **and Rydal Water** ($\frac{3}{4}$ by $\frac{1}{4}$). Here are reedy lake shores, with a backing of deciduous woodland. Both

Grasmere and Rydal Water attract large numbers of coot and black-headed gull in the winter. Mallard, whooper and mute swans are also to be seen. White Moss Common, near Rydal, a nature walk of about 45 minutes' duration, by woodland and open fell, has been arranged by the National Trust and the Lake District Naturalists' Trust. On the walk may be seen tree-creeper, dipper, grey wagtail, pied flycatcher. A leaflet is available.

A view above the village of Rydal.

Grizedale Forest (8,000 acres). Grizedale, a Forestry Commission holding, lies between Coniston and Windermere; the offices and wildlife museum are two miles south of Hawkshead, on the Hawkshead-Satterthwaite main road. The area holds 5,700 acres of coniferous plantations and 718 acres of broad-leaved woodland. The main tree block is centred on the Grizedale Valley but outliers extend northwards to Tarn Hows, eastwards to Claife and southwards to Nibthwaite and Newby Bridge.

Several nature trails of short duration can be followed. A tougher expedition, of $9\frac{1}{2}$ miles, the Silurian Way, is named after the underlying rock formation. The way begins at the wildlife centre, which should first be visited. The Silurian Way can be covered comfortably in a short day or, if more convenient, in two stints, though some of the going is rough and the weather is always uncertain; stout footwear and adequate protective clothing are recommended wear. The Ridding Wood Nature Trail, of a mile, can be completed in an hour.

43

Haweswater ($2\frac{1}{2}$ by $\frac{1}{2}$) **and Wet Sleddale**. The former Mardale was flooded as a reservoir by Manchester Corporation (a body which is, incidentally, being sympathetic to wild bird life). In more recent times Haweswater has been linked, by a tunnel cut through the fells, to a newer reservoir in Wet Sleddale.

Haweswater's horse-shoe of fells at its head include High Street and Kidsty Pike. An autumn migration route for ringed plover and dunlin follows High Street and a good number of birds have been seen there in September. Naddle, on the southern side of Haweswater, is an extensive area of oak forest.

Fellside nesting birds include kestrel, ring ouzel and a few black grouse. In Naddle Forest are buzzard, green and great spotted woodpeckers, garden and wood warblers, blackcap, pied and spotted flycatchers and woodcock. Among the waterside species are mallard, teal, common sandpiper, red-breasted merganser.

Haweswater has a winter roost of black-headed and common gulls, totalling about 12,000 birds. Typically, the gulls divide into rafts of 1,500—2,000 each of the same species. The roost breaks up in April. In that month lesser black-backed gulls might be seen. There may be 500 roosting black-headed gulls in early July, with common gulls arriving in small numbers before the end of the month.

Wet Sleddale is, as the name implies, a good place for snipe, and in this valley have nested oystercatcher and ringed plover.

Leighton Moss (about 400 acres). The Moss, formerly arable land, in a wooded valley between Silverdale and Yealand Redmayne, has been a Royal Society for the Protection of Birds Reserve on lease since 1964. Permits are needed for special hides (obtainable from the R.S.P.B., The Lodge, Sandy, Bedfordshire) but there is unrestricted access to a central causeway and to a hide standing beside it.

Four shallow meres are edged by dense reed swamps, with more open fen edge in drier parts; and here there are sedges and rushes, with some willow and alder. An area of willow scrub exists at the head of the valley. At Leighton Moss, 182 species of bird have been recorded and 70 species have bred. The only regular breeding pairs of bittern in northern England are found here. Bearded tit nested in 1973. Water rail breed commonly and winter in the reserve; reed warblers are abundant, and sedge and grasshopper warblers can invariably be seen. Woodland birds include green and great spotted woodpeckers.

The public causeway at Leighton Moss. Dense reed swamps at Leighton hold several pairs of bitterns.

Leighton is well-known for its large population of wildfowl—mallard, teal, shoveler, with smaller numbers of pochard, tufted duck and garganey. Pintail, wigeon and gadwall have "summered" on the reserve. A colony of about 250 pairs of black-headed gulls nests on the Moss and many herons fish in the meres.

The reed beds are used by large flocks of roosting birds. Starlings occur in number from July to March, and swallows and sand martins on migration roost in spring and from July to September. Migrant waders are attracted to the muddy areas within the refuge in spring and autumn. Wintering wildfowl include mallard (up to 2,000) shoveler (100-200), teal (500), wigeon (varying in successive years from 30 to 200). Tufted duck, pochard and goldeneye are regular visitors from October to April.

Eaves Wood Walk, Silverdale, arranged by the National Trust and the Lancashire Naturalists' Trust (leaflet available) starts near St. John's Church, Silverdale. This former coppiced area contains the common woodland birds, including treecreeper, green and great spotted woodpeckers. Woodcock are mainly seen in winter.

Loweswater (see Buttermere).

Lowther Wildlife Park (150 acres with three acre lake). The Park, situated near Penrith, includes much old beech, oak and sycamore. The pied flycatcher is locally common; some pairs use nest boxes. (It was at Lowther that Dr. John Heysham, of Carlisle, studied the species in the 1780s). Also present is the spotted flycatcher. Other nesters are great spotted woodpecker, redstart, reed bunting, lapwing, curlew, with little grebe on the lake. The deciduous woods attract nesting woodcock. Buzzard and sparrow-hawk may be seen. Ravens are heard calling far above as they migrate between the Cumbrian and Pennine fells.

Martindale. Instead of progressing to the dalehead, by a road running close to a river or beck, the entry point for Martindale is over a steep ridge, the Hause, near Howtown, by Ullswater. Martindale itself is divided by the Nab into two small valleys—Bannisdale (west) and Rams Gill (east). A by-road serves Boredale and another road decends to the hamlet of Sandwick by Ullswater. Ravens nest at traditional sites on crags. Buzzards use the "hanging" woodland. Wheatears are relatively common but there are few ring ouzels. Dippers, feeding in the fast-flowing streams, sometimes nest on the undersides of bridges. A pair of stonechats was seen in February, 1973.

Meathop Moss. This reserve by the Kent comprises two mosses (Meathop and Catcrag). It is approached by a road leaving Grange-over-Sands. The area is leased as a nature reserve by the Lake District Naturalists' Trust; a permit is needed for entry. Meathop is a raised peat bog that developed on estuarine silt; the moss is drying out as a consequence of drainage on adjacent agricultural land. Look for buzzard, kestrel, five species of the tit family, redpoll, goldcrest, and treecreeper. The district holds willow warblers, fewer grasshopper warblers and some tree pipits.

Patterdale. The valley is situated between the northern end of Kirkstone Pass and Ullswater. The fells are well-wooded on their lower slopes, and meadows and patches of marshy ground lie by the river. Extending from Patterdale are a number of small, craggy dales. Ravens nest on the crags, which traditionally also held a pair of kestrels, and sparrow-hawks are reported. Some buzzards are tree-nesters, but others nest on crags, at between 1,500 and 1,800 feet above sea level. Tawny owls are locally common; the barn owl is present and has been recorded as a cliff-nester.

The wheatear, a common summer visitor to the Lake District, where it frequents open country, extending its nesting range to most of the fell tops.

Pied flycatcher nest in old woodland, where nesting boxes have been distributed by the Lake District Naturalists' Trust. (A pioneer scheme for introducing nest boxes was organised 40 years ago by Dr. Moon, of Glenridding, and continued by J. R. Cooper). The kingfisher has returned to the riverside following a natural decline of the species caused by the inclemency of the 1963 winter. Swallows and house-martins occur at the farmsteads.

Brotherswater (1 by $\frac{1}{4}$) is a small and comparatively shallow lake fringed by reed. Mallard nest here, but larger numbers of this species are seen from October to December. Wigeon, goldeneye, pochard and tufted duck occur outside the nesting season. Up to 30 coot have been recorded, and small parties of whooper swans sojourn in winter. Also observed at Brotherswater are heron, shelduck, and oystercatcher. It is known from nocturnal calling that grey geese, mostly greylag, alight in the vicinity of the lake during foggy weather.

Roudsea Wood (287 acres).   Sprawling by the Leven estuary, the wood has a variety of habitats including sessile oakwood, ashwood and yew-wood on limestone and slate, raised bog, mixed fen and west coast saltmarsh. Bird species recorded as breeding on the reserve include mallard, shelduck, sparrowhawk, woodcock, curlew, tawny owl, green and great spotted woodpeckers, marsh tit, redstart, blackcap, garden warbler, whitethroat, chiffchaff, bullfinch, yellow hammer. Inquiries about access should be made to the Nature Conservancy, Merlewood, Grange-over-Sands.

Rusland Valley. The area in which Rusland lies is dominantly woodland and there was much coppicing here in the past. The pied flycatcher is a characteristic bird. Rusland Moss (58 acres) has been a national nature reserve since 1955 and here is one of the few remaining examples in southern Lakeland of a moss that has not been damaged beyond repair. The reserve is part of a raised bog only 20 feet above sea level which originated in a shallow lake. Although partly cut and drained, the moss retains most of the characteristic bog plants and animals. A permit is required. Apply to Merlewood Research Station, Grange-over-Sands.

The Hay Bridge Nature Reserve and Deer Museum is open to school and natural history society parties on prior application (Hay Bridge, Booth, Ulverston). One of the items in the *Hay Bridge File* concerns the birds of the area (a radius of 15 km, comprising farmland, deciduous woodland, coniferous forest, wetland, lakes, rivers, high fells, estuaries saltmarsh and the sands of Morecambe Bay). Species seen on the Hay Bridge Nature Reserve, on which no detailed survey has yet been made, include heron, greylag, shelduck, sparrow-hawk, buzzard, snipe, woodcock, barn and little owls, green and great spotted woodpeckers, redstart, grasshopper warbler, yellow hammer, jay.

Rydal Water (see Grasmere).

Staveley. The village is by the Kendal-Windermere road. Nearby is Dorothy Farrer's Spring, a reserve of the Lake District Naturalists' Trust. A degenerate mixed coppice wood covers about $3\frac{1}{2}$ acres on a south-facing slope. A nature trail considered suitable for upper primary school pupils has been laid out; an instruction leaflet is available. Birds to be seen in

The jay at its nest. The Lakeland population of this species is mainly found in the southern woodlands.

this area include jay, kestrel, magpie, goldcrest, tree-creeper, tit family (including the long-tailed). Kentmere, which is entered from Staveley, is an isolated valley terminating with the crags of Thornthwaite, Harter Fell and Lingwell End. Froswick and Ill Bell divide Kentmere from the upper Troutbeck valley.

Tarn Hows. (The name, used for tarn and the area about, came from Tarnhouse, a nearby cottage). Water, woodland

and craggy fells make up a familiar scene. When a dam was constructed about 1865 "The Tarns", three in number, were merged into one. A nature walk around Tarn Hows has been arranged by the National Trust and the Lake District Naturalists' Trust; a leaflet is available. The one and a-half hour walk begins and ends at a large, free car park. Apart from the birds usually frequenting a large coniferous environment, you may see buzzard and raven. The carrion crow is ubiquitous. Moorhen, mallard and coot are among the water birds and greylag geese nest on an island. Yellow hammer and stonechat favour local juniper bushes.

Thirlmere valley. This area has a wide variety of habitats, from high wet moorland to low fertile pasture. There is also felltop and crag, almost every type of woodland, lake, stream and tarn. Some 60 species of birds breed there, and many other species can be seen occasionally. More than 100 nest boxes are maintained. As long ago as 1912 there were 370 boxes in the newly-planted forests, of which 75% were occupied—as today—mainly by tits, pied flycatchers and the occasional redstart. (In the early days, extensive feeding "trays" of hessian were laid out on the snow, and the seed from the haybarn floors was swept up and put out in hard weather).

Thirlmere itself is always worth a glance, but the lake shore is, unfortunately, still a forbidden area. Some 50 Canada geese (and the occasional greylag) spend their flightless summer here. Broods of goslings are raised at the southern end. To see geese, stop near Wythburn church, and look over the wall. Geese are usually present in this area.

In general, there is no objection to people wandering at large on land above the roads, though most would wish to follow a path of some sort. On the east side one can only safely park at the back of Wythburn Church, where the Helvellyn path commences, or at the car park on the top of Park Brow, about a quarter of a mile south of the *Kings Head* inn at Thirlspot. From here another path starts up Helvellyn and a visitor can wander along the Swirls Forest Trail through mixed woodland to a pleasant viewpoint.

From the starting post of the Swirls Trail, a newly-opened footpath leads northwards along an open aqueduct to plunge down and cross the main road at the *Kings Head* through open pastures skirting the woodland on Great How, crossing St. John's Beck by the old bridge and then over the fields again and across Shoulthwaite Moss. Here a visitor can use a bus on the main road or hitch a lift back to the starting point. The new

Thirlmere, as views from Raven Crag.

footpath is part of a long-distance route being made through the valley. In 1975 it should be possible to walk right through the forest on the Helvellyn slope, well clear of the sound of traffic, to rejoin the A591 on Dunmail Raise.

To investigate the west side of Thirlmere, cross the dam and park at the triangle. Half-an-hour of hard walking is needed to reach the top of Raven Crag, or Castle Crag Fort, an Ancient British encampment, in a commanding position looking down the Shoulthwaite Valley.

Half a mile south, at the first lay-by, a visitor can commence half-an-hour's gentle tour of an area of Douglas fir and visit the biggest silver fir in northern England. Bird-watchers usually get neckache from watching birds on branches nearly 150 feet above.

At Armboth there is the prospect of following a footpath on the open fell, or making a more gradual ascent through wood-land to Fishercrag. The Launchy Gill Forest Trail leads a walker about half way up the valley side to the Tottling Stone. Great spotted woodpeckers can be seen in this area. Another walk begins at the foot of the Harrop woodlands and ascends to Harrop Tarn, which is set about with spruce. In summer, swifts snatch flies from the tarn's surface. A sparrow-hawk may be seen.

Bird species that have been seen in the Thirlmere Valley in recent times include:

Woodlands and rides – Crossbill, tree-creeper, four species of the tit family, pied flycatcher, redstart, goldcrest, great spotted and green woodpeckers, sparrow-hawk, woodcock, jay, tawny and barn owls, goldfinch, bullfinch. *On the lake* – Canada goose, greylag, mallard, teal, tufted duck, goosander, red-breasted merganser, cormorant, Bewick's swan. *Along St. John's Beck* – Dipper, grey and pied wagtails, common sand-piper, heron. *In the air* – Raven, buzzard, peregrine falcon, kestrel, merlin. *Wet fell* – Snipe and red grouse. *Dry fell* – Skylark, meadow pipit, wheatear.

Thornthwaite Forest (5,000 acres). The Forest, which lies around Bassenthwaite, north of Keswick, belongs to the Forestry Commission. Sitka spruce and some Scots pine grow at 1,000 feet beside Whinlatter Pass (High Lorton to Keswick area). A forest trail and walks take in Dodd Wood. (Car park by the A591 four miles north of Keswick.) A leaflet gives the walks in detail, with maps and line drawings. Buzzard, raven and tawny owl are among birds breeding in the area. The golden eagle and osprey have been seen in this district outside the nesting season.

Ullswater (8 by 1). The second largest lake in the region, Ullswater has a maximum depth of 205 feet. A notable orni-thological feature of Ullswater is a winter gull roost, referred to elsewhere. The lake is a good place for wildfowl in winter. Goldeneye are among the species seen and cormorants turn up to feed.

The teal is most commonly seen in eastern areas. It breeds on the Shap Fells.

Whitbarrow. Here, on a high limestone plateau, is the Hervey Nature Reserve of the Lake District Naturalists' Trust, commemorating Canon G. A. K. Hervey, founder of the Trust. Approach from Lyth Valley (The Howe). An illustrated leaflet is available. Adjacent land is being managed as a reserve by the R.S.P.B., South Lakeland Group. The breeding birds of Whitbarrow include skylark, meadow and tree pipits, cuckoo, willow warbler, tit family, green and great spotted woodpecker. Among the species seen are nightjar, black grouse, raven. Two woodland species of special interest are buzzard and woodcock.

Windermere (10½ by 1). The largest of the Cumbrian lakes, Windermere has a north-south line. The head of the lake lies among high fells and the tail is not far from the sands of Morecambe Bay. Reedy bays on the eastern side of Windermere include Rayrigg and White Cross. Other notable bays for bird-watchers to overlook are Pull Wyke and High Wray. The wintering waterfowl include the whooper swan (up to 30 birds), tufted duck, goldeneye, goosander, grebes, occasionally divers, a few pochard and teal. Cormorants are frequently present and non-breeders arrive on Windermere during the nesting season. The breeding species include red-breasted merganser, mallard, coot, moorhen and mute swan. Among the birds of the Windermere woodlands are pied flycatcher, chiffchaff, garden and willow warblers, blackcap, redstart, marsh tit.

A Claife Shore Walk of nearly 1½ miles was arranged by the National Trust and the Freshwater Biological Association. A descriptive leaflet is available. Belle Isle, opposite Coatlap Point, is the largest island in the lake and provides sanctuary for many water birds including red-breasted merganser, mallard and coot. The island is private. Windermere is a halting place for whooper swans on their journey south in early winter from Iceland and Scandinavia.

Wastwater (3 by ¾). Wastwater's grandeur is derived partly from the Screes, which are some 1,700 feet high (the average slope being 45°). Nether Wasdale Nature Trail, 3½ miles in length, was arranged by the Lake District Naturalists' Trust, partly on land belonging to the National Trust. Generally, it is around the outflow of Wastwater; a descriptive leaflet is available. Local birds: buzzard, raven, peregrine falcon, green and lesser spotted woodpeckers, goldcrest, dipper, black-headed gull, mallard and greylag.

Opposite page: Black-headed gulls hover at the edge of Wastwater, with Great Gable providing a grand background to the view. At Nether Wasdale is a three and a-half mile nature trail.

Migration

Hardly any serious research had been undertaken into the bird migratory patterns of inland Cumbria until local members of the R.S.P.B. undertook useful field work. Older records contain much relevant information.

Migration in Lakeland is largely governed by the existence of mountain barriers which, in places, exceed 3,000 feet. Some birds migrate over the ridges, but most choose to follow the natural "funnels"—the passes and dales. Some of the dales are conveniently on a north-south axis.

Greylags which are not, on the whole, in large numbers, appear to use two flyways from the Solway area to Morecambe Bay. The usual way is via the Eden Valley and the Lune; the other is a central route via Bassenthwaite Lake (where they usually briefly touch down), Thirlmere (another halt) and over Dunmail Raise to southern Lakeland.

Most greylags are of Icelandic origin but some are Scottish birds, and greylags originating at the Haws reserve, near Millom, have been recovered from Ayrshire, where they were in the moult. Other Millom birds have consorted with geese in Perthshire. A greylag goose from Millom was shot in Iceland.

In the 1950s, skeins of pinkfeet passed regularly down the Eden valley towards the eastern part of the country. The flight-line could be traced from the Rockcliffe Marsh area of the Solway, along the edge of the Pennines, west of Dufton, then diagonally over the A66 road between Appleby and Warcop, towards Nine Standards Rigg, which lies west of Stainmore. This direction would take the geese to the Humber and the Wash. Grey geese have been seen on this route only occasionally in recent years.

Pinkfeet geese regularly use five principal routes from the Solway to Morecambe Bay and points south and east:

(1) The Eden Valley and the Lune, as above. These are usually birds which have congregated near the Rockcliffe end of the Solway.

56

(2)   Birds which assemble near Rockcliffe Point tend to move south and east of Wigton and the Skiddaw-Saddleback range, where they gain height and pass well up over the Kirkstone Pass area to the Windermere valley and south. It would seem that very seldom do these birds touch down until they reach the marshes.

(3)   Birds which assemble on the Newton Arlosh or Skinburness marshes move slightly west up the Aikshaw valley, then fly either just to the east or over Aspatria, Bothel, over Bassenthwaite Lake (where occasionally some touch down for a while) and Thirlmere (where again a few touch down, but not many). In the main, the birds gain height and continue via the Windermere valley until they reach the marshes.

(4)   This is a semi-coastal route, with birds flying down the Solway, coming inland to the west of Silloth, west of Aspatria, over Cockermouth area, over Ennerdale and Gosforth to the Muncaster Marshes, where they usually touch down for several hours, thence overland to the Duddon.

(5)   The last is a complete coastal route with the primary passage of birds flying from the Rockcliffe Marsh area via Caerlaverock. They then move south-west, coming into Cumbrian waters to the north of Maryport. Some of these birds touch down for a feed near Seaton, but in the main they keep about a mile off shore, coming into half a mile at St. Bees where, however, they do not loiter. Some geese alight on the Ravenglass Marshes, but in the main they appear to continue south by passing the Duddon and South Walney and, it is presumed, heading for the Southport area.

All of these routes have been followed and monitored by car and boat regularly during the past few years. Routes 1, 2 and 3 take the birds to heights of 4,000 feet at times; route 4 to 2,000 feet; and birds on route 5 keep to about 500 feet above the water all the way. The greatest activity on all routes is during late September and through October. In the spring return passage, the flylines are still used, in reverse direction, but numbers of birds are more spread out. Weather factors also produce a good deal of coming and going between the Solway and Morecambe Bay, mainly by route 4.

Pinkfeet moving in fair numbers in late September and April have been noted in southern Lakeland, with 53 birds moving south on November 5, 1971; 42 birds going north on December 21, 1971; 156 south on September 25, 1972 and 118 birds passing south over Sizeergh, February 26, 1973.

The flyways are undoubtedly used, at various altitudes, by other large passage migrants—waders, gulls, terns—but such species have far more positive flyways of their own, mostly at the coast.

The barnacle goose, a generally marine species, has been protected by law for some years and a considerable rise in the British wintering population is noted. Slightly over 5,000 wintering barnacle geese now winter on the Solway. This is not a Lakeland species as such, but a few birds occur now and again at lakes. They do not appear to have any special flyway, and few birds seem to leave the Solway area, but some barnacles join up with skeins of pinkfeet and move around Lakeland in the winter months. All-white barnacles are occasionally recorded on the Solway.

The barnacle geese wintering on coastal Cumbria have been proved to originate in Spitzbergen. Barnacle geese reared at The Haws, near Millom, are believed in due course to migrate north with wild stock. Young birds may accompany grey goose flocks into Lakeland. The only recovery of a barnacle goose in Lakeland, as opposed to the coast, was at Sawrey, near Hawkshead. A bird was killed when it collided with an overhead wire.

The saw-billed ducks, mainly goosanders but also a few red-breasted mergansers, pass up the Eden in autumn in greater numbers than are recorded for such traffic in the opposite direction. It is presumed the birds cross from the Kirkby Stephen area to Ravenstonedale, joining Lunesdale and continuing to Morecambe Bay, thus avoiding the higher fells.

Of the other wildfowl, a tufted duck ringed as a young bird at Sunbiggin Tarn in June was shot in the following autumn at Wexford, Eire. A goldeneye from Sweden was shot at Windermere one and a-half years after being ringed. Wigeon from the nests of stock introduced via a reserve at The Haws (Duddon estuary) have been recovered from the Baltic States, Scandinavia (Lapland and Sweden) and Russia. Gadwall ringed at the same reserve were slain in Eire and France. A mute swan ringed as a full-grown bird at Barrow-in-Furness on July 21, 1965, was "controlled" as a male while breeding at Ormside, Appleby, in 1969, and in the following years up to 1973.

Black-headed gulls, after nesting in Lakeland, disperse to many points. RWR has ringed several youngsters in the Eden Valley area that were later recovered from the estuaries of Duddon and Kent. A black-headed gull chick ringed at

The Haws, near Millom, showing some of the grey geese that have been reared here. Shelduck and wigeon nest in the woods of this district.

A pink-footed goose, nesting in good cover at the Millom reserve which, incidentally, is on private land.

Ravenglass on June 12, 1965, was found dead at Horse Island, Ardrossan, on June 4, 1967.

Waders are great travellers. There have been fairly frequent reports of whimbrel being heard in Lakeland dales during the spring and late summer. Whimbrel are fast flyers and observations suggest that almost all use the coastal route on a spring migration which is usually undertaken quickly and within a mile or so of the coast. Most whimbrel will pass through Cumbrian coastal waters in two hours or so. On autumn passage, birds of this species still keep to the coast but, with frequent stops, probably take several days to pass through coastal Cumbria.

Curlew movements are most interesting. During late June and early July the breeding populations from parts of Lakeland and the western Pennines appear to move to the coast, with adults marshalling their chicks via fields and stream valleys, the adults watching from the air. At dawn in early July there is great activity on many parts of the Cumbrian coast, particularly the Solway, as those families which have survived the journey finally get to the shoreline. They break cover and make for the safety of the sandflats.

In July very large flocks indeed can be found on the Solway and on the west Cumberland coast. These birds feed up and appear to move away by the end of July. In late August birds from points north and east begin to move into the Solway; Lakeland and the fells are now deserted. The curlews form into large flocks feeding on the sandflats and adjacent marshes. These flocks can be traced, moving westwards all the time, until they arrive at the principal exit point near Siddick, where they feed for a while, assemble and then move out to sea, gaining height en route before overflying the Isle of Man and on to Ireland.

Manx bird-watchers have co-operated with Cumbrian ornithologists in studying this flight-line. No great flight-line of curlews through Lakeland has been found, but there is a conspicuous night movement during the autumn, as evidenced by the calling of many birds as they move south over towns and villages. The main movement is, however, coastal.

Calls are heard at night as curlews pass over such Lakeland towns as Kendal, Penrith and Appleby. A large passage of curlews over Kendal took place on the evenings and during the nights of March 20, 1969 and March 14, 1972. In other years this passage was spread over several nights in mid-March.

The ringing of lapwings in the Lake Counties indicates a similar strong movement of the species to areas south and west of their breeding places, most birds wintering in southern Ireland. Some lapwings apparently travel further south than curlews, going to France, and Spain. Others reach Wales or southern England during the winter.

The lapwing, a common breeder in Lakeland, has even taken advantage of territories provided by grassed-over traffic "islands" where road improvements have been made. This bird was incubating eggs in the rain.

Of a more local nature, Cumbrian ravens cross the valley heads from one range of fells to another, and communal roosting occurs at favourite crags in winter. Young birds and non-breeders flock in summer. A passage of Cumbrian ravens to the Pennines, which is observable at points in the Eden Valley, has already been commented upon. A raven ringed at High Cup Nick, on the northern Pennines, on June 24, 1963, had its ring recovered on Scafell on June 13, 1964.

An autumnal sight in Lakeland dales where the rowan is common, is a congregation of thrushes—mistle, song and blackbird. They dine on berries while this convenient source of nourishment lasts. Some thrushes may form itinerant flocks of locally-bred birds, but ringing has indicated that Continental birds are regularly present.

When the fieldfares and redwings arrive, about October, some make use of the crop of haws left on the hedgerows and isolated trees growing on the slopes of the fells. These northern thrushes cross the Cumbrian fell ranges and move about the dales in winter, their journeys being related to the availability of food. Recent observations suggest that the principal movement of fieldfares and redwings is within, say, 10 miles of the coast. Relatively few birds move into Lakeland.

Redpolls and siskins, arriving in large numbers from northern Europe, are attracted by alder and birch. Bramblings are notoriously unpredictable; the species can be present in large flocks at times when beech mast abounds. In the hard winter of 1963, bramblings tended to leave the higher ground, assembling in the valley bottoms.

All birds migrate to a degree. Many of the birds that breed in Lakeland move to the coast during the winter. Short migrations are undertaken by birds that have nested in exposed areas; they go to more sheltered parts. Peregrine falcons, for instance, may move to lower crags or they may go to the coast, which is also the wintering place of many northern merlins.

A kestrel ringed as a nestling at Sandford, Appleby on June 25, 1971, was found dead at Holehird, Windermere on November of that year, but two other Edenvale nestlings were shot in France.

Ringing the legs of birds yields much valuable and often surprising information. An oystercatcher ringed at Flookburgh on February 16, 1964, was found dead at Hamburg six years later (*British Birds*). An Uldale-ringed young redshank was recovered in Devon four months later. Herons are usually thought of as being sedentary, but Scandinavian herons winter in this country. A heron ringed at Vastergot, Sweden, was recovered at Rampside, Furness, a year later. A Norwegian nestling heron was ringed, and the bird recovered 10 months later at Satterthwaite in High Furness.

A cormorant ringed as a juvenile at the Farne Islands, and another cormorant ringed in Wigtonshire, were caught in gill nets put out in Windermere by the Freshwater Biological Association.

Visual observations have their part to play in fixing migration patterns. Of the unexpected reports was one of six Arctic terns seen feeding at Whinfell Tarn, near Kendal, in May, 1972. A peregrine falcon roosted regularly at the atomic station at Winscale during part of a summer and on into winter. It made regular forays to the Drigg gullery at nesting time, and its daily kills were traced by the plucking of feathers.

Waxwings are believed to enter Lakeland via the Tyne Gap, also via the Nith Valley (Dumfriesshire) and across the Solway. Twenty-five waxwings were seen in a garden at

Bassenthwaite on November 9, 1957. Waxwings were well distributed in Lakeland during an "invasion" in December 1958 and January, 1959.

Wrecks of oceanic birds are signified by recoveries well inland. The remains of a Manx shearwater were picked up at the top end of the Kentmere valley in January, 1968. This bird is believed to have been killed by a peregrine falcon. A razor-bill turned up at Langholm and a guillemot on the A6 at Shap in January, 1972. In October, 1956, an injured gannet was found at Underbarrow, Westmorland. Presumably, like the shearwater, the gannet had been blown inland by high winds.

The kestrel is a well-distributed resident species.

A Few Wintering Species

VISITORS unfamiliar with Lakeland should look carefully at swans seen in the shallows of the lakes in winter. Not all will be the relatively common mute swans. Whooper and Bewick's swans come to winter in the district. Whooper swans, many of Icelandic origin, are most numerous.

Whoopers are seen regularly from the middle of October until April. The parties generally are small, consisting of one or more family groups. The juveniles are readily distinguishable because their plumage is greyish. White feathers are assumed after the second winter, though some grey feathers are to be seen until the following year.

Among the "swan lakes" is Elterwater, and birds are attracted especially to an area near Rob Rash Wood, where the Brathay flows out of the lake. Grasmere, Rydal, Bassenthwaite, Coniston, Windermere, Thirlmere and Harrop Tarn are visited by the northern swans. When high tarns have frozen over, Derwentwater is popular. The late Dr. Moon, who lived at Glenridding, believed that swans could not live for more than a few weeks on Ullswater. It was suspected that poison from Greenside lead mine was concerned, but no proof of mineral poisoning could be found.

Ullswater is notable for the vast numbers of gulls roosting here in autumn and winter. Late each evening large flocks of gulls are seen flying down the Eden Valley to converge on the lake. W. Atkinson, writing in the February 1949 issue of *The Lakeland Natural History News-Letter*, which he edited, stated that on January 28, 1949, there were about 3,000 gulls, including 10 lesser black-backed gulls and two great black-backed gulls. On a February evening, he reported that thousands of gulls had settled. Hundreds more birds were joining them. Only herring and black-headed gulls were recognisable from the shore, but Mr. Atkinson thought that common gulls must also have been present. Observations made at Patterdale showed a movement down the line of the valley to the lake each night.

Ullswater, which is outstanding for the size of its winter gull roosts. In January, 1973, a count revealed about 12,000 common gulls and 2,500 black-headed gulls.

from Bassenthwaite and Ennerdale. Thirty cormorants were seen on Haweswater on December 26, 1972. The goldeneye is another familiar wintering species.

An issue of the *Field Naturalist* (March, 1955) quotes a note from J. C. Cooper, of Glenridding. He estimated 2,000 to 3,000 common gulls in the middle and upper reaches of Ullswater, as well as 300 common, 100-150 herring and 500 black-headed gulls near Pooley Bridge. It was a much smaller assembly than was the case some years later when the estimate was 15,000 - 20,000 gulls.

Gull counts on Ullswater by RWR in September, 1959, indicated about 4,500 common gulls, 2,500 black-headed gulls and 100 lesser black-headed gulls. A count on Ullswater in December, 1963, revealed 4,500 - 5,000 black-headed gulls, 8,000 - 10,000 common gulls, 250 lesser black-backed gulls and 50 herring gulls.

Recoveries of ringed gulls revealed the places of origin. Two common gulls had been ringed as young birds in Norway. A black-headed gull was ringed as young in Poland. Another of the same species had been ringed at Colchester. Birds from local gulleries—Sunbiggin Tarn and Kirkby Thore—also roosted on Ullswater.

Haweswater is the setting for another big gull roost. On January 14, 1973, a count on Ullswater revealed approximately 12,000 common gulls, 2,500 black-headed gulls, 25 lesser black-backed gulls and 2 herring gulls. At Haweswater, on January 28, were 7,000 common gulls, 2,500 black-headed gulls and 15 lesser black-backed gulls.

Bassenthwaite Lake has a large winter gull roost. There is another on the Kent estuary, the birds being mainly common gulls in winter, black-headed gulls in summer. An estimate by M.H. indicated around 2,000 to 5,000 birds. A count of 20,000 plus, mainly common and black-headed gulls, was made by A.F.G. on September 12, 1973. An estimated 2,400 black-headed gulls occupied part of Millerground Bay, Windermere, in November, 1956, and December, 1957.

Winter is the most rewarding season for observing wildfowl on the lakes and tarns. Species to be seen are pochard (especially on Derwentwater and Bassenthwaite Lake), mallard and teal (look especially at Rydal, Esthwaite, Elterwater, Bassenthwaite). There were 250 coot on Ullswater on January 14, 1973. and up to 1,000 have been counted on Windermere. The velvet scoter has been observed on Windermere (five birds on November 18, 1952).

Above: A herring gull at its nest. Left: Nesting colony of black-headed gulls. Below: A great black-backed gull takes flight.

Check List

THIS is a selective list, mainly of birds that a visitor might see, given time—and luck. The local names for birds (CN for Cumberland, WN for Westmorland) are from a glossary compiled by Macpherson and Duckworth in 1886. Apart from their quaintness, these names are often expressive of some important features of the birds.

RED-THROATED DIVER (*Gavia stellata*)
(CN - speckle-backed diver)
The commonest of the wintering divers, the redthroat is seen on the lakes in hard weather, the three most favoured lakes being Windermere, Ullswater and Haweswater. It has been reported from Devoke Water, above the Duddon. A bird was found dead beside Esthwaite Water in March, 1964. There is a red-throated avian highway about three miles out in Cumbrian waters and up into the Solway in spring.

BLACK-THROATED DIVER (*Gavia artica*)
Winter visitor, especially in hard weather. Has been observed on Windermere and also the much smaller Devoke Water. A bird was picked up alive in a snow-covered field at Temple Sowerby, Edenvale, in January, 1970; it was released on Ullswater by J. S. Marshall.

GREAT NORTHERN DIVER (*Gavia immer*)
A winter visitor, most often reported from Windermere, though six birds were seen on Ullswater by J. Cooper in January, 1953.

LITTLE GREBE (*Tachybaptus ruficollis*)
Most widely distributed of the grebes and found on most suitable stretches of water. Little grebe is a resident of lakes,

tarns, and ponds, up to an elevation of about 1,000 feet. The species has nested at the head of Ullswater, on which lake it has increased in number as a wintering species. It also occasionally winters on the Kent.

BLACK-NECKED GREBE (*Podiceps nigricollis*)
Bred in Westmorland in 1935 and again in the 1960s. A pair was seen on Coniston Water in May, 1973.

SLAVONIAN GREBE (*Podiceps auritus*)
Off-season birds have been seen on Windermere, Grasmere and Haweswater.

GREAT-CRESTED GREBE (*Podiceps cristatus*)
Once found only at Esthwaite Water and Blelham Tarn (where it nests), this grebe has now spread to remoter sites, but it remains very local. Nesting took place on Whinfell Tarn, Westmorland, in the 1960s. Has bred by Coniston Water, Overwater, Bassenthwaite Lake. Winter visitors are observed, especially at Esthwaite Water.

CORMORANT (*Phalacrocorax carbo*)
(CN - scart)
Feeds regularly on the larger lakes, such as Bassenthwaite Lake, Thirlmere, Windermere, Ullswater, Crummock Water, Haweswater and Coniston Water. The species is most often seen in winter, and parties of cormorants roost on islets with trees. Thirty birds were seen roosting on Haweswater in December, 1972; 20 on Roughholme Island, Windermere, through the winter of 1957/8, and there was a further roost on Fir Island, Coniston Water. G.L.W. recorded up to 127 cormorants in the Duddon estuary, and some of these were believed to fish in Seathwaite Tarn, Devoke Water and Coniston Water.

SHAG (*Phalacrocorax aristotelis*)
An uncommon species inland. A nestling from Sutherland was recovered from Windermere in the following December.

HERON (*Ardea cinerea*)
(CN - heronsue, Willy Fisher)
Resident. The largest heronries are found in the southern dales adjacent to Morecambe Bay, which offer abundant food. Breeding haunts elsewhere include Muncaster and a point near Keswick. The heron is not always a colonial breeder.

Single nesting pairs have been reported. Herons of Norwegian origin have been recovered in southern Lakeland.

BITTERN (*Botaurus stellaris*)

Up to nine nesting pairs at Leighton Moss, 1973, and one or two pairs on nearby Haweswater. A bittern was reported seen at Bassenthwaite Lake in 1959, and at the head of Coniston Water in 1971 and 1972. Single birds have been observed on the western shore of Windermere and by the river Mint, north of Kendal.

MUTE SWAN (*Cygnus olor*)

Resident. Census for 1955-6 by BTO, giving 33 nests for Lake Counties, was probably incomplete. The species has bred on Bassenthwaite Lake, Derwentwater, Windermere, Coniston and Ennerdale Lake.

The whooper swan, a winter visitor to Lakeland, arriving in late October. The last birds depart in late April.

WHOOPER SWAN (*Cygnus cygnus*)

A winter visitor. First sightings are usually in late October. Birds may still be seen in Lakeland in late April. The "swan lakes" include Windermere, Grasmere, Derwentwater, Thirlmere, Elterwater, Ennerdale Water, Bassenthwaite Lake, Coniston Water, Devoke Water. The species is also reported from Leighton Moss, Whinfell Tarn and the reservoir near the Garburn Pass. Flocks of up to 40 birds have been reported in recent times. Kirkby Thore, Edenvale, has a wintering group, and the maximum number was 74 in February 1973. Up to 45 had been counted two years earlier.

BEWICK'S SWAN (*Cygnus bewickii*)

Winter visitor, usually seen from November onwards. Bewick's swan is less common than the whooper swan in our region. The Bewick is attracted to some of the lakes patronised by whoopers. Has been reported from Wastwater and Ullswater (3 birds near Pooley Bridge in January, 1973). A single bird tried to alight in a gull roost at Haweswater in early April, 1971, but was driven off by gulls. Occasionally, a pair of Bewick's alight on Devoke Water. The Foulshaw and Meathop mosses, by the Kent, are attractive to the species. Nine birds were seen on Ratherheath from November 16 to 27, 1972.

PINK-FOOTED GOOSE (*Anser fabalis*)
(CN - pink legs)

The pinkfoot has become the commonest winter goose on Solway, and small numbers annually associate with the greylag flock on the Kent estuary. Lakeland is traversed by migrants using several flyways. (See the section on migration).

WHITE-FRONTED GOOSE (*Anser albifrons*)

Uncommon winter visitor. Regular in small numbers on the Solway. Nine birds visited Sunbiggin Tarn, Westmorland, for several days in early March, 1961. A single bird, of the Greenland type, was seen at Watersmeet, Culgaith, with greylags, in November, 1972.

GREY-LAG GOOSE (*Anser anser*)

Resident, with a large and rising breeding population originating from eggs of Scottish birds hatched out at The Haws, near Millom. Most greylag colonies are on lakes in the north and west of the region; the total Lakeland population is estimated at 400. A winter flock of over 1,000 greylags (with a few pinkfeet) occurs at Watersmeet, near Culgaith, and this flock has built up from c400 birds in February, 1958. The Kent estuary wintering flock of about 300 birds is the most southerly for greylags in Britain. The numbers have fluctuated in recent years; if anything they have declined.

CANADA GOOSE (*Branta canadensis*)

The species has bred successfully at several Lakeland tarns, and is locally increasing in number. A breeding flock uses Killington reservoir, near the M.6., and 32 birds were present in April, 1972, with 35 in September, 1973. A thriving flock can be seen at Lowther Wildlife Park. The Canada goose nests at Whin's Tarn, Edenhall.

The Canada goose, which is becoming more numerous.

BARNACLE GOOSE (*Branta leucopsis*)

Birds of Spitzbergen origin winter in coastal areas of Cumbria, notably Solway. Barnacle geese have been reared at The Haws, Millom. Birds were believed to have bred at Buttermere in the 1960s, but were later reported as Canada geese. Single bird at Watersmeet, Culgaith, early April, 1972; two at Foulshaw, Kent Estuary, in September, 1973.

SHELDUCK (*Tadorna tadorna*)
(CN - shell duck, gravel duck)

Resident. Nesting population of around 300 occurs on the Duddon estuary, with nesting taking place on slopes above the Whitcham Valley, one and a-half miles from salt water. Birds of Duddon origin may be those often seen at Boretree Tarn and High Dam, above the river Duddon. The shelduck also nests in the Rusland Valley and beside Windermere, but there was a population decline about Windermere, two contributory factors being the incidence of myxomatosis (which led to a dearth of rabbit burrows suitable for shelduck nesting) and increased tourism. A pair of shelduck bred by Rydal Water in 1963.

WIGEON (*Anas penelope*)
(CN - lough duck, lough teal)
100 or 200 wigeon at Leighton Moss in most years. The species is the commonest wintering duck on the Cumbrian coast, being far less common at this season on lakes and tarns. Reported from Bassenthwaite Lake, Devoke Water, Bigland Tarn. The wigeon has been well-known as a breeder over past 20 years. Pairs bred at Sunbiggin Tarn, Westmorland, from 1944 and 1973. A scheme for breeding and releasing wigeon, begun at The Haws, near Millom, in the 1960s, led to the species breeding wild in the vicinity of the Duddon estuary.

GADWALL (*Anas strepera*)
Breeding took place at a Westmorland tarn in 1973 and previous years back to at least 1958. The species is present at Leighton Moss.

TEAL (*Anas crecca*)
Resident, also winter visitor. Most commonly seen in the eastern areas, with breeding on Shap Fells and on the gentler slopes of Place Fell, Ullswater. Also breeds in High Furness. Wintering parties on the river Lowther.

MALLARD (*Anas platyrhynchos*)
Mallard, the commonest of the Lakeland ducks, can be found on lakes and tarns throughout the region, including Windermere, Coniston Water, Devoke Water, Grasmere, Rydal Water, Esthwaite Water, Brotherswater, Little Langdale Tarn, Beacon Tarn, Boretree Tarn, Bigland Tarn, and on rivers. Is locally very common where there are rearing schemes, and it retains its high numbers despite increased shooting pressures. Nesting takes place on the Lakeland fells up to 1,200 feet. Mallard flighting to the stubble near the estuaries, especially Kent and Duddon, have in recent years been joined by pintails. The species moves into Lakeland in quite large numbers in late July and early August.

SHOVELER (*Anas clypeata*)
(CN - grey duck)

Has bred at several high-lying tarns, where it is not as common as formerly. Nesting occurs in Northern Lakeland and at Leighton Moss.

POCHARD (*Aythya ferina*)

A winter visitor, regularly reported from Loweswater, Bassenthwaite Lake, Coniston Water, Whinfell Tarn (where there were 22 birds in October, 1964) and Fisher Tarn, the last two in Westmorland. A raft of 100 birds was seen on Rydal Water in February, 1952. The pochard has nested at Leighton Moss.

TUFTED DUCK (*Aythya fuligula*)

Resident, winter visitor. The tufted duck breeds at several high-level tarns and at Leighton Moss. A bird ringed at Sunbiggin Tarn in June, 1953, was shot at Kilmore, Wexford, Eire, in February, 1954. As a winter visitor, the species is fairly common on most open waters.

GOLDENEYE (*Bucephala clangula*)
(CN - whiteside)

Winter visitor, in small numbers, to a number of lakes. Largest numbers are seen in spring, just before northerly migration to the nesting areas. Forty-six birds were counted on Blelham Tarn, west of Windermere, in April, 1961.

SMEW (*Mergus albellus*)

An occasional winter visitor, reported from Coniston Water, Bassenthwaite Lake, Ullswater, Windermere, Kitmere Tarn near Kirkby Lonsdale, and Leighton Moss.

RED-BREASTED MERGANSER (*Mergus serrator*)
(CN - sawbill)

Remarkable increase in numbers, with a spread in recent decades to many parts of Lakeland. This merganser had become well-established by 1971. It is particularly common on Windermere, where sizeable groups of birds can be seen in late summer, and it has bred by Coniston Water, Crummock Water, Bassenthwaite Lake, Haweswater and Ullswater. A number of pairs are reported from the lakeless Eskdale. At Windermere, the food preference is for small perch. The red-breasted merganser is also a winter visitor.

74

GOOSANDER (*Mergus merganser*)
(CN - goosandrew)

Breeding species and winter visitor. Increasing number of breeders at riverside locations, also at Bassenthwaite and in the Shap Fells area. Up to 40 goosanders have been seen on Ullswater in winter.

OSPREY (*Pandion haliaetus*)

Passage migrant. Lingering birds seen by Bassenthwaite Lake, Ullswater, at confluence of Rydal Beck and Rothay, by Ennerdale (1973) and Devoke Water (a bird stayed for five days in the winter of 1972). More than one osprey may be seen in a good year at Leighton Moss. The best viewing season here is from early May to late June.

MARSH HARRIER (*Circus aeruginosus*)

Rare vagrant. Leighton Moss is a fairly frequent point of call and a possible future nesting area. The species is seen occasionally on Ulpha Fell.

HEN HARRIER (*Circus cyaneus*)

The hen harrier has bred in recent years on fells in north-central Lakeland. Rare sightings of hen harriers at Leighton Moss.

SPARROW-HAWK (*Accipiter nisus*)
(CN - blue hawk)

The Lakeland sparrow-hawk population has not been as gravely affected as those in other parts of the country. Now the species is relatively common again, often nesting in conifer woods. Breeding sites include Ennerdale area, west of Windermere and about Leighton Moss.

COMMON BUZZARD (*Buteo buteo*)
(CN - shreak)

Resident with about 50 nesting pairs in Lakeland. Most numerous on the southern and western edges of the region. Common in Lyth Valley, Kendal, and around the estuary of the Kent. The buzzard has reverted to tree-nesting, with birds moving to woods and Forestry Commission sites on lower ground. There are an estimated seven pairs in the Grizedale area of High Furness.

GOLDEN EAGLE (*Aquila chrysaetos*)

Rare resident, and for long simply a vagrant. Empty nest found 1957, first eggs 1969, nesting successes in 1970, 1971, 1972. Eaglet hatched but died, 1973. Typical eagle country is the central fell area, but hunting sorties take place to lower hills, where food is more easily obtained. A golden eagle might, by chance, be seen anywhere in the area.

KESTREL (*Falco tinnunculus*)
(CN - red hawk).

Resident, well distributed. Tree-nesting up to about 1,700 feet (the kestrel frequently uses the old nests of magpie and carrion crow), with cliff-nesting up to 2,000 feet. This species is the commonest of the birds of prey, being seen in all areas except the highest fells, and especially on fellsides, in the dales and in lowland and wooded areas. The kestrel has its highest population in "vole years", the most recent being 1971.

MERLIN (*Falco columbarius*)
(CN - small blue hawk)

Resident, quite scarce, nesting on moorland. Nests are generally found at elevations up to 1,700 feet, though in 1971 merlins nested at 1,900 feet. Merlins are seen by the coastal estuaries in winter.

PEREGRINE FALCON (*Falco peregrinus*)

Resident, about 20 pairs. Nests on crags, generally between about 1,500 feet and 1,750 feet. There are records of nesting at over 2,000 feet. Lakeland birds tend to either shift their quarters to more sheltered crags or move to low country and the coast in winter.

CAPERCAILLIE (*Tetrao urogallus*)

Resident, following an introduction of Scottish birds to Grizedale Forest, in High Furness. First recorded nesting occurred in 1973, but this attempt was unsuccessful. The capercaillie has tended to move eastwards, from the forest proper, towards the more lightly wooded country around Esthwaite Lake.

BLACK GROUSE (*Lyrurus tetrix*)

Resident, local, in diminishing numbers. Lekking in the Troutbeck (Greystoke), Coniston Water and Shap Fells areas. Black grouse reported from the Ennerdale district, Solway Mosses and also Bannisdale.

RED GROUSE (*Lyrurus lagopus*)

Resident, local. Can be common on heathered areas, which are mainly found at the periphery of Lakeland, especially in the north and east.

PARTRIDGE (*Perdix perdix*)
(CN - Patrick)

Resident. Decline in numbers reported from some areas, but there has been a substantial revival in others since 1969. Fairly common in the Lowther valley and other broad eastern dales. Sportsmen once considered the fell-going partridge to be generally smaller, greyer, than that on low land.

PHEASANT (*Phasianus colchicus*)

Resident, from latter part of 18th century. Introduced and is reared for sport, but wild-nesting reported from many lowland areas. A flourishing colony of pheasants was seen at the northern end of Haweswater in 1971; one female was sitting on 23 eggs.

WATER-RAIL (*Rallus aquaticus*)

Resident. This skulking species occurs in areas of fen, including Bassenthwaite, Leighton Moss, nearby Hawswater, Blelham Tarn and a reservoir near Kendal. A water-rail found in the ski hut at the top of Sticks Pass, at 2,500 feet, in October, 1960, had gained entry through snow grid.

CORNCRAKE (*Crex crex*)
(WN - daker hen)

Summer visitor, now a rarity. Bred successfully at Brigsteer, in the Lyth Valley in 1971. Was heard at Gatesgarth (Buttermere) in 1955, Old Brathay in 1961, by the Keswick/Bassenthwaite stretch of railway in 1962, near Hawkshead in 1967, near Thursby in 1970 and on farmland at Bampton (three singing males) in 1971, in which year the corncrake was also heard calling in Uldale. Nesting near Scales in 1972 and in both the Caldbeck and Keswick areas in 1973. Up to 1950, the species was often heard at Longlands, Kendal.

MOORHEN (*Gallinula chloropus*)
(CN - waterhen)

Resident, by quiet waters—ponds and streams, up to an elevation of about 1,000 feet. Congregations of moorhens are found on the main valley lakes in winter.

COOT (*Fulica atra*)

Resident, winter visitor. Nests on all the main lakes and also a number of tarns, including Blelham. Wintering parties can be large on lower lakes. Over 850 coot were seen on a reach of Windermere in February, 1952, and winter population is now even higher. The species is common in winter at Leighton Moss.

OYSTERCATCHER (*Haematopus ostralegus*)
(CN - sea piet)

Visitor for breeding, sometimes using ploughed fields on high ground. More usually nests at tarn edges. The oystercatcher, which is common on the Cumbrian coast, is not well-distributed in the central areas of Lakeland.

LAPWING (*Vanellus vanellus*)
(CN - tewfit, peesweep)

This common breeder on open ground showed an alarming decrease in numbers from the middle 1950s, but is recovering well. There was a flock of 3,000 lapwings at Foulshaw, by the Kent estuary, in September, 1973. A lapwing ringed in Patterdale by Dr. Moon in May, 1926, was recovered in Newfoundland in December, 1927.

GOLDEN PLOVER (*Pluvialis apricaria*)

Nests sparingly on the Lakeland fells, and is much commoner on the nearby Pennines. The species prefers to nest on broken ground of a rolling nature, at around 1,000 feet. Golden plovers can be seen on Shap Fells, Skiddaw Forest and some western moors. There was a winter flock of cl,500 birds by the Kent estuary in March, 1972.

RINGED PLOVER (*Charadrius hiaticula*)
(CN - sea bellet)

The ringed plover is of comparatively rare occurrence along any of the lake shores. A pair bred in Wet Sleddale in 1971. This species is quite common as a nesting species on the coast. Nesting regularly takes place by the Duddon estuary, from which birds fly as far inland as Seathwaite Tarn to feed and roost.

DOTTEREL (*Eudromias morinellus*)

Rare and intermittent breeder on the *Rhacomitrium* heath and high stony plateaux, customarily above 2,400 feet. "Trips" of dotterel were relatively common in lowland Lancashire, but none of more than four birds has been seen here since 1950.

CURLEW (*Numenius arquata*)
(CN - whaup)
The curlew nests in reduced numbers on moors up to 2,600 feet; also, in more recent years, on farmland in the lower dales. Curlews nest near the heads of most lake-filled dales where suitable open marshy ground exists. Nesting took place in the centre of an oakwood at Matson Ground, Windermere, in 1959, and the species has nested in areas recently planted with conifers. Upwards of 40 pairs nest each year within the area of the Duddon valley

REDSHANK (*Tringa totanus*)
(CN - redlegs)
Breeds on damp ground up to 1,500 feet. The species is increasing in number and the nesting range is being extended in Lakeland. A winter roost of over 50 redshanks on Kendal warehouse roofs in 1972 and 1973 was noted by JMSA.

GREENSHANK (*Tringa nebularia*)
Passage migrant, frequently on high ground. Birds also visit tarns and lakes, as well as coastal areas, during passage.

COMMON SANDPIPER (*Actitis hypoleucos*)
(CN - willie liltie, summer snipe, sandy piper)
Summer visitor. Well-distributed by lakes and tarns, also streamsides at up to 2,000 feet, though the nesting site is generally at a lower elevation. The sandpiper is quite successful despite tourist pressures. Birds nesting by the rivers frequently have their nests swept away by floodwater.

COMMON SNIPE (*Gallinago gallinago*)
Resident, winter visitor. Pennine birds tend to nest at high elevations, but in Lakeland snipe usually choose the marshy "bottoms" of the dales. There was an autumnal gathering of up to 800 snipe at Leighton Moss in 1971, and great snipe was seen here in September, 1959.

WOODCOCK (*Scolopax rusticola*)
Resident, autumn visitor. The nesting of woodcock in Lakeland has been reported for rather more than a century and now the species is quite well-distributed in wooded areas. Nesting on bare ground, on Grizedale Pike, has been recorded. Immigration of Continental birds about October.

DUNLIN (*Calidris alpina*)
(CN - sea mouse)

Uncommon breeder, usually ignoring the central fells, preferring rolling country where there are pools of marshy places. Nesting site preferences are generally similar to those of the golden plover; hence the name "plover's page."

COMMON GULL (*Larus canus*)

Winter visitor, with large roosts on some lakes. Many long and regular flylines from Lakeland to the coast are used in winter. About 12,000 birds roosted on Ullswater on January 14, 1973. About 7,000 were seen on Haweswater a fortnight later.

HERRING GULL (*Larus argentatus*).

There are visits by non-breeders from coastal areas, where many thousands nest, to the dale country.

LESSER BLACK-BACKED GULL (*Larus fuscus*)

Non-breeding visitors to the dales from coastal areas. Small numbers (20-50) on large lakes, notably Ullswater and Haweswater, in winter. A wintering roost is being formed near Keswick. A few birds of this species overwinter in Kendal, feeding in the town during the day and flying out of town to roost.

GREAT BLACK-BACKED GULL (*Larus marinus*)

Visitor from the coastal areas. Up to 20 birds were seen on the east shore of Ullswater in November, 1961 (R. Stokoe). GLW has recorded up to 50 birds in the Duddon estuary; they were obviously birds of passage, the average daily count over seven years being 10. Up to eight birds roost around Devoke Water, and occasionally a few birds are seen at Seathwaite Tarn. The species was recorded at Stickle Tarn in 1970. Each autumn there is a migratory movement of great black-backed gulls through and around Lakeland. Groups of up to 250 birds have been seen.

BLACK-HEADED GULL (*Larus ridibundus*)

Drigg, on the Cumbrian coast, has a major black-headed gullery. Many smaller nesting colonies have been established at the periphery of the area of fells. Lakes are used for roosting purposes. In January, 1973, an estimated 2,500 gulls roosted on Ullswater and there was a similar number on Haweswater. Among many ringing recoveries was that of a nesting ringed in Poland in June, 1958, and found dead by Ullswater in September, 1961. Cumbria appears to be host in winter to some Continental birds.

STOCK DOVE (*Columba oenas*)
(CN - Scotch cushat)

Fairly evenly distributed as a nesting species on lowlands and lower fell crags. Deserted farm buildings are frequently used for nesting.

WOODPIGEON (*Columba palumbus*)
(CN - cushat)

Conifer plantations encouraged woodpigeons to increase in number, but the population varies in accordance with the availability of food. The bird feeds freely on acorns and beech mast in season. Immigrant pigeons in winter include some Scottish birds.

COLLARED DOVE. (*Streptopelia decaocto*)

Resident. Now common in parks and gardens. A population explosion was noted in 1973. The first collared dove seen in the Kendal area was in Parkside Cemetery in the spring of 1967; now the species has spread to all parts of the town. Nesting occurs generally throughout lowland Lakeland.

CUCKOO (*Cuculus canorus*)

Fairly common, widespread visitor for breeding. The cuckoo is a prominent bird on the fellsides in spring, and it can be locally very common in quieter Westmorland dales. Generally, however, the species is not as common in the region as it was 30 years ago.

BARN OWL (*Tyto alba*)

Resident, local. The size of the barn owl population has been much reduced during this century, most notably from about 1965. Breeding is reported from Derwentwater and Windermere areas, but most surviving pairs nest in the south-western area, some quite close to the estuaries. The presence of barn owls in the eastern areas is testified by road casualties. A barn owl was picked up dead on the M.6 north of Penrith on April 1, 1973; a second bird was a road victim in the same area on April 29. In 1973, a barn owl flew into the windscreen of a slow-moving car using the Whitcham Valley road in the south-west.

LITTLE OWL (*Athene noctua*)

Resident. The first breeding record for central Lakeland was in about 1944. Some evidence exists of the continuing spread of the species, and more daylight sightings have been noted. A pair breeding in the Heversham district, not far from Kent estuary, in 1973, chose as the site a hole at the base of a wall.

Tawny owl carrying a worm to its offspring.

TAWNY OWL (*Strix aluco*)
Resident. The commonest of the owl species. Well-distributed. Some woodland nests at over 1,000 feet.

LONG-EARED OWL (*Asio otus*)
Resident, uncommon. Nests in several small pine woods on Cumberland fells, the woods being at an elevation of 1,100-1,200 feet (R. Stokoe).

SHORT-EARED OWL (*Asio flammeus*)
Visitor for breeding; now uncommon, but population can rise strikingly in "vole years". This owl breeds in the Killington area of Westmorland. A bird observed at Sunbiggin Tarn, on the Westmorland fells, plunged into a roost of swallows in reeds on September 20, 1973. Winter sightings are possible.

NIGHTJAR (*Caprimulgus europaeus*)
(CN - night hawk)
Visitor for breeding, with decreasing numbers. Some recent sightings in the Keswick area (1959 and 1960). Esthwaite

(1958), Cartmel Fell (1961), Arnside, Duddon Valley (where it has bred since 1967), Finsthwaite Heights and Kirkby Moor. The species bred on a coastal moss by the Kent in 1972 and in West Cumberland in 1973.

SWIFT (*Apus apus*)
(CN - devilen)

Visitor for breeding. The nest is sited under eaves of old houses in towns and large villages. Swifts frequently seek winged insects over the highest fells, and large numbers seen over High Street in July, 1971, were probably breeders from Penrith.

KINGFISHER (*Alcedo atthis.*)

The kingfisher population has made a good recovery following a serious natural decrease in the 1963 winter. The species is especially common on the southern and western rivers and becks.

GREEN WOODPECKER (*Picus viridus*)

The species is more widespread in Lakeland than it was a few years ago. A significant extension of the nesting range took place from the south in the 1940s, with the spread taking in the Kent and Duddon valleys and the east side of Windermere. The green woodpecker is now to be seen in many old woods, and also in park-like country (open, but quite well wooded) around Keswick, Bassenthwaite and Ennerdale Bridge.

GREAT SPOTTED WOODPECKER (*Dendrocopos major*)

This resident in woodland with aged or dead timber shows a preference for deciduous trees, especially silver birch, in the eastern area. The great spotted woodpecker is common in the Windermere and Ullswater basins, and it has bred in the Derwentwater area. Trees chipped by the great spotted woodpecker can be found within the town of Kendal.

LESSER SPOTTED WOODPECKER (*Dendrocopos minor*)

This resident, mainly found in the southern part of Lakeland, appears to be extending its range. Sightings near Grange-over-Sands, Lyth Valley, near Kendal and, according to Yapp (1951), at Howtown, Ullswater.

SKYLARK (*Alauda arvensis*)

Fairly common and widespread visitor to the hills for breeding. The skylark prefers gentle, grassy slopes, with the result that it may be common on some fellsides, absent from others.

Young swallows in a Lakeland barn.

SAND MARTIN (*Riparia riparia*)

Visitor for breeding, but least common in the central fell area. At Kendal, sand martins have nested in blocked drains in walls and by a bridge over the Kent.

SWALLOW (*Hirundo rustica*)

Visitor for breeding. The swallow is largely dependent on farm outbuildings. A swallow was seen passing the summit of Scafell Pike.

HOUSE MARTIN (*Delichon urbica*)

Visitor for breeding, but with numbers no more than half of those 20 years ago. Like the swallow, the species is largely dependent on buildings for nesting sites. As this is the crucial factor, some martins nest at over 1,000 feet where buildings exist. Nesting sites reported include the "steamer" landing at Pooley Bridge (Ullswater) and a building in Highgate, the main street of Kendal, which was used in 1973. House martins feed on winged insects high on the fells. Pre-migration gatherings may be seen in early August.

YELLOW WAGTAIL (*Motacilla flava*)

Visitor for breeding. Local. The yellow wagtail prefers wet meadowland and rough pastures in fell districts. Nests may be found at elevations up to about 1,000 feet. Although commonest in some of the eastern valleys, the yellow wagtail is represented at the heart of Lakeland—for instance, around Seathwaite, head of Borrowdale, where the fields are at little more than 400 feet above sea level. A decline in numbers comparable to figures over the rest of Britain was noted in 1973.

GREY WAGTAIL (*Motacilla cinerea*)

Visitor for breeding; but a few birds overwinter in the region. The grey wagtail, common along fast-flowing rivers and streams, often nests in the close company of the dipper. The overwintering of a few birds has been reported from the river Kent, between Kendal and Burneside.

PIED WAGTAIL (*Motacilla alba*)
(CN - watery wagtail; WN - watty)

This is the commonest of the wagtail species in the Lake District National Park. It is common in valley and fellside situations, with nests at elevations up to about 2,000 feet. Pied wagtails tend to flock around lakes before autumn migration. A few birds overwinter. There is a noticeable return passage of birds in early April. A factory roof at Netherfield, Kendal, was used as a roost for three nights by 22 birds during stormy weather in November, 1964. About 700 roosted at Appleby Express Dairy in April, 1970, when there was a cold spell. This roosting place was used in subsequent springs but by much smaller numbers of birds.

TREE PIPIT (*Anthus trivialis*)

Visitor for breeding, being characteristically a bird of the upper dales, especially where trees are thinly spread. The tree pipit can be locally common, but the population has decreased in some areas.

MEADOW PIPIT (*Anthus pratensis*)
(CN - titling, moss cheeper; WN - ling bird)

Most abundant of the fellside species, nesting at almost 3,000 feet in central Lakeland. Some overwintering is reported, but the majority of meadow pipits are absent at this time and return to the fells in March, often in quite large flocks that split down into several parties, then into pairs. Most breeders quit the fells after rearing the young. The meadow pipit is a common host to the eggs of the cuckoo, and a common victim of a hunting merlin.

WAXWING (*Bombycilla garrulus*)

Occasional winter visitor, following irruptions from the Continent. Among the sightings of recent years were 15 birds behind Kendal Grammar School, November 5, 1965; 9 in the same area, January 18, 1966; 3 at Temple Sowerby, December 3, 1970; 10 at Sizergh Castle, December 16, 1970, and also a single bird here on December 26, 1971; 5 at Temple Sowerby, November 16, 1972; 4 at Natland, Kendal, December 2, 1972.

DIPPER (*Cinclus cinclus*)
(CN - Bessy Dooker, water crow)

Resident. The dipper is common where there are becks and fast-flowing rivers. Most nests are found below an elevation of 1,500 feet, but nesting at over 2,000 feet has been reported. Dippers at the highest-situated nests tend to follow the becks still higher to feed.

The dipper, one of the most distinctive of the Lakeland birds. This species thrives where there are fast, clear streams. It nests far up on the fells as well as in the sheltered dales.

WREN (*Troglodytes troglodytes*)
(CN - chitty)

Resident, well-distributed, from dales to the highest crags. The wren is, quite often, the only bird to be seen on the highest ground in winter.

DUNNOCK (*Prunella modularis*)
(CN - dykey, creepie dyke)

This shy species can be seen in every Lakeland valley through-out the year. There is an especially large population in the Rusland Valley, to the south of the region. Although mainly residental, a notable passage is reported from the verge of Lakeland in spring and autumn.

ROBIN (*Erithacus rubecula*)

Resident. Common and widely distributed in wooded areas. Some evidence has been gathered to indicate a movement of Lakeland birds away for the winter and the occupation of parts of Lakeland by birds from Scotland and the Continent.

REDSTART (*Phoenicurus phoenicurus*)

Summer visitor, breeding up to the tree line. Holes in rotten trees are frequently used, but the redstart also nests round farm buildings and in drystone walls on lower ground. Nest boxes are readily accepted. A numerical decline of redstarts has been reported from some areas in recent years.

WHINCHAT (*Saxicola rubetra*)
(CN - utick;   WN - gorsechat)

Visitor for breeding, well distributed. In some areas, including Haweswater, a preference for bracken and gorse is noted. The species is fairly common around Ennerdale Lake; it has bred near Bassenthwaite.

STONECHAT (*Saxicola torquata*)

Now local. Was well-distributed at many inland sites up to 1,600 feet but became uncommon as an inland breeder after the hard winters of the 1940s. Signs of a numerical recovery inland are evident. A pair was seen in Bannisdale on February 18, 1973. Another pair wintered by Killington reservoir in 1971 and 1972. Meanwhile, the stonechat is at present mainly confined to the coastal strip.

WHEATEAR (*Oenanthe oenanthe*)
(CN - white rump)

Common summer visitor. Frequents open country, extending its nesting range to most of the fell tops. Is abundant where there are drystone walls, but also uses rabbit burrows. The wheatear arrives at the end of March, being one of the first of the spring migrants to appear. Birds of the northern race, from Greenland, are regular passage migrants in late April and May; also in September and October.

RING OUZEL (*Turdus torquatus*)
(CN - fell throstle, mountain crow)

Summer visitor, nesting at elevations up to 2,500 feet, but mainly up to about 1,750 feet. The ring ouzel appears to be most common in Lakeland on crags covered by bilberry, such as the spurs of High Street. Has been recorded for many years as nesting on Walna Scar, Dow Crags and Old Man. Parties of ring ouzels feed on berries along the fellsides before migrating to North Africa. The overwintering of a few birds is suspected.

BLACKBIRD (*Turdus merula*)
(CN - blackie)

This common breeding bird in areas up to about 1,000 feet is said to have a range extending to a point at which the ring ouzel ("mountain blackbird") takes over. In fact, the ranges of the two species overlap in places. The bird is least common on the fellsides; it prefers wooded areas. Sometimes, where a wood has no shrub layer and is at a high elevation, it will nest on the ground. A late nest with young, in Castle Road Cemetery, Kendal, was found on August 4, 1971.

FIELDFARE (*Turdus pilaris*)
(CN - bluewing, felfaw)

Winter visitor, passage migrant. Can be numerous. The West Cumberland Field Society saw c40 birds at the summit of Pillar Mountain in late September. A flock of c750 was seen flying through Bannisdale and circling around the Nab in October, 1973. During the cold springs in 1972 and 1973, fieldfares appeared to delay their return to the nesting grounds in Scandinavia. In spring, 1973, they were in particularly large numbers. An estimated 2,600-plus seen at Helsington on April 9 was not unusual.

REDWING (*Turdus iliacus*)
(CN - felty)

A winter visitor, redwing is less conspicuous in numbers than the fieldfare, with which it consorts, especially towards the end of the winter. A Lakeland bird was heard in song in June, 1958 (*British Birds*).

SONG THRUSH (*Turdus philomelos*)
(CN - throstle)

A common and widespread nesting species.

MISTLE THRUSH (*Turdus viscivorus*)
(CN - churr cock, mountain throstle)

Fairly common on the lowlands, and also at home on the high fells. Nesting occurs among the crags at up to 1,500 feet.

GRASSHOPPER WARBLER (*Locustella naevia*)
(CN - grasshopper lark)

This visitor for breeding is unusual above 500 feet. The year 1973 was particularly good for the nesting of this species in the Duddon valley; for instance, six pairs bred successfully in the scrub of the Frith Hall area. The grasshopper warbler has also been recorded as breeding in the Rusland Valley, Bigland Tarn and Burnmoor Tarn districts, and at Leighton Moss.

SEDGE WARBLER (*Acrocephalus schoenobaenus*)
(CN - water nannie)

A visitor for breeding, with a preference for dense vegetation near water, the sedge warbler is quite common in suitable areas. There was an estimate of 350 singing males at Leighton Moss in 1968.

GARDEN WARBLER (*Sylvia borin*)

The garden warbler is fairly common in some woods and gardens, mainly in the valley bottoms, and the species has possibly become more widespread in recent years. Breeding takes place in the Duddon valley, Rusland Valley, Broughton Mills valley, Newby Bridge district and the eastern side of Coniston Water.

BLACKCAP (*Sylvia atricapilla*)

This visitor for breeding is not common. Among its northern nesting haunts is Naddle Forest, above Haweswater.

WHITETHROAT (*Sylvia communis*)
(CN - peggy, nettle creeper; WN - streasmere)

Visitor for breeding. The species was very common in hedge bottoms, nettle beds and similar sites where there is rough vegetation. The whitethroat is now local, being absent from sites where herbicides have been used, though this is not considered to be the main reason for the decline. The lesser whitethroat, *Sylvia curruca,* is very local in distribution, but its numbers may not have fallen to the extent of the whitethroat. The lesser whitethroat bred at Levens in 1972.

WILLOW WARBLER (*Phylloscopus trochilus*)
(CN - bottlety, miller's thumb)

Visitor for breeding, and the commonest of all the visiting warblers. The willow warbler is also the most generally distributed warbler. Its breeding range extends right up the fells to the tree line.

CHIFFCHAFF (*Phylloscopus collybita*)

Visitor for breeding, spasmodically distributed but heard on early spring migration as it passes through the dales. Birds were heard singing in September at Bassenthwaite (1954), Heversham and Sandside (1973).

WOOD WARBLER (*Phylloscopus sibilatrix*)

Visitor for breeding. Local. Ranges up to nearly 1,000 feet in suitable areas. Breeds in Patterdale, Duddon and Rusland Valleys; also in Naddle Forest, Haweswater.

GOLDCREST (*Regulus regulus*)

Resident. Winter visitor. The goldcrest is fairly common in coniferous plantations, but may also be seen in woodland with varied tree species. State forests favour the species and have made a considerable rise in the population possible. The goldcrest is, however, vulnerable to hard winters.

PIED FLYCATCHER (*Picedula hypoleuca*)
(CN - lal or little magpie)

Visitor for breeding. Local, but can be common in old deciduous woodland, and especially common where there are nest box schemes, such as in Grizedale Forest (High Furness). Possibly most common in the southern Lakeland valleys, although a pair nested in Bannisdale in 1973.

SPOTTED FLYCATCHER (*Muscicapa striata*)
(CN - French robin)
Visitor for breeding. Widespread, and common where there is open woodland. The range of the spotted flycatcher extends to an elevation of about 750 feet.

LONG-TAILED TIT (*Aegithalos caudatus*)
Resident. Nests where there is good tree cover, even on the lower slopes of the fells. Nomadic flocks (frequently with others of the tit family) in winter.

WILLOW TIT (*Parus montanus*)
Occurs over most of Cumberland, except the south and east. The species has penetrated into the fell country as far as Derwentwater.

MARSH TIT (*Parus palustris*)
The marsh tit is confined to mature woodland, and the population remains even. It is locally common in southern Lakeland. A pair of marsh tits bred at Ratherheath in 1973.

COAL TIT (*Parus ater*)
The species is common wherever there are pine trees and it attains a higher elevation at nesting time than other members of the tit family.

GREAT TIT (*Parus major*)
(CN - blackcap)
The great tit is common in most stretches of woodland, except those at the highest elevation, though the species has been found at around 1,000 feet. Flocking of great tits with other members of the tit family and other small woodland birds (tree-creeper, goldcrest) occurs in winter.

BLUE TIT (*Parus caeruleus*)
(CN - bluecap)
Resident, being the commonest of the Lakeland tits. The blue tit can be found in all wooded areas and gardens.

NUTHATCH (*Sitta europaea*)
Resident, local, uncommon. The nuthatch has been reported from Ullswater, Rydal, Grasmere, Skelwith Bridge, and a bird was seen feeding young in Grizedale Forest in 1961. A pair bred in Levens Park in 1973.

TREE-CREEPER (*Certhia familiaris*)
Resident in areas of well-grown timber, including coniferous plantations. Some urbanisation noted; a bird was seen on a tree near Nether Bridge, Kendal, in the spring of 1959, and the species is common in many such places.

CORN BUNTING (*Emberiza calandra*)
(CN - bunting lark)
Resident, local. The species favours a few traditional areas, from which it does not seem inclined to extend its range. It has tended to be associated with arable areas, and with barns where grain was threshed. Birds could thus feed during the winter on vast reserves of weed seed left by the thresher. Corn buntings are found in fair numbers near the Kent estuary.

YELLOW HAMMER (*Emberiza citrinella*)
(CN - yellow yorling; WN - Bessy Blakeling)
Resident, relatively common, being associated mainly with areas of bracken; breeding proved at up to 1,000 feet. Flocks of yellow hammers are noted in winter.

REED BUNTING (*Emberiza schoeniclus*)
(CN - reed sparrow)
Mainly resident. Local distribution. Some birds return in March, with nesting occurring in marshy areas—around lake shores, even on some islets.

LAPLAND BUNTING (*Calcarius lapponicus*)
Uncommon winter visitor. There are only four records for Lakeland, including a male at Derwentwater in May, 1959. The species is usually seen in the company of snow buntings on high ground.

SNOW BUNTING (*Plectrophenax nivalis*)
(CN - fell sparrow, snow bird)
Winter visitor. The central fells of Lakeland, on which parties have been seen, are generally less attractive than some Pennine fells. A flock of 40 snow buntings was seen at Troutbeck in November, 1962. In the previous winter, 10 birds were observed near Coniston in January and 20 on Helvellyn in March. In some fell areas, snow buntings are attracted to hay being fed to sheep in times of snow.

CHAFFINCH (*Fringilla coelebs*)
(CN - scoppie, shiltie)

Resident and common. Becomes tame in places where it is regularly fed by visitors, an example being a much-used car park. A pair of chaffinches in Borrowdale regularly built their nest with cigarette filter tips. About 100 chaffinches were seen at Whinfell in April, 1965, but parties of wintering birds are generally much smaller than this. Nesting occurs in woodland up to about 1,500 feet. The chaffinch is generally distributed in coniferous areas. Evidence of influx of Continental birds on autumn migration.

BRAMBLING (*Fringilla montifringilla*)
(CN - cock o' the north)

Winter visitor to the dales, generally from October, but is absent in some years. The brambling is attracted to stands of beech, and 150 birds were seen foraging beneath trees of this species in Natland Road, Kendal, in January, 1972. Up to 30 bramblings were counted in a greenfinch roost in December, 1971, in which month 65 birds were observed at Sizergh Castle.

GREENFINCH (*Carduelis chloris*)
(CN - greenie)

Resident, both in woodland and gardens. Also a winter visitor, some of the flocks being quite large.

GOLDFINCH (*Carduelis carduelis*)
(CN - goldie)

Resident, on low ground, frequently in gardens. Much attracted to areas where thistles abound. Has become quite common around Kendal, where it bred successfully in 1971. The Lakeland population has been increasing in recent years.

SISKIN (*Carduelis spinus*)

Uncommon breeder, though it has bred in Grizedale and by Haweswater. The siskin is more commonly observed as a winter visitor, from October until about March, when a flock of from 20 to 30 birds might be seen. Such flocks are generally on alders by water.

REDPOLL (*Acanthis flammea*)

Resident, breeding (quite late in the season) in deciduous scrub, also among young conifers. Common in al! suitable locations. As a winter visitor, it tends to converge where there are birch and alder trees. (The mealy redpoll has been recorded in Lakeland). Most records are for the period from November until February.

TWITE (*Acanthis flavirostris*)
(CN - heather lintie)

A few pairs nest in the Lake Counties. Recorded mainly in winter. There are records of twite being seen on Birker Fell, Corney Fell, High Street and Ullscarf. A scattered party of 6-plus was seen in Borrowdale (Westmorland) on April 15, 1972. The twite was seen and heard in Ennerdale Forest early in July, 1957.

LINNET (*Acanthis cannabina*)
(CN - grey, whingrey)

Resident, winter visitor. Is found mainly on low ground, or lower fell slopes, especially where gorse provides sites for nesting and roosting. Nests have been found in fell country at up to 1,200 feet. A nest found in Spital Woods, near Kendal, in the spring of 1972, had the lining material added following the laying of the first egg. A.F.G. carefully disentangled the egg from this material and, visiting the nest a week later, found the hen sitting a full clutch. Flocks of linnets move into the higher breeding areas in late April and early May. The species appears to be less common in Lakeland than it was.

CROSSBILL (*Loxia curvirostra*)

Immigrant, occasional nester. Has recently bred in three places in Westmorland, also near Thirlmere and near Keswick. The crossbill has benefited from the maturing of large tracts of coniferous forest. A maximum of 300 birds was noted in one such area in mid-October, 1956. A male was picked up dead on Whinlatter in January, 1964. Since the 1950s, crossbill flocks have been seen at Skiddaw Dodd, Thirlmere, at the foot of Whinlatter, Claife Heights (above Windermere), and between Ambleside and Skelwith Bridge (where there are many larch trees).

BULLFINCH (*Pyrrhula pyrrhula*)

Resident. Of local distribution, but fairly common around Kendal. Bullfinches are most often seen in southern Lakeland; there are sporadic flocks in autumn and winter.

HAWFINCH (*Coccothraustes coccothraustes*)

Resident, locally distributed in deciduous woodland, mainly

southern Lakeland (around Windermere, Coniston Water, Elterwater). Has been reported from near Bassenthwaite. A pair nested in the Lyth valley in 1972 and 1973. Hawfinches appear to favour damson-growing areas.

HOUSE SPARROW (*Passer domesticus*)
(CN - sprug)

Resident, common where there are groups of buildings. The house sparrow is a familiar bird in the dales where small villages and farms provide nesting sites and food is easily obtained in winter.

TREE SPARROW (*Passer montanus*)

Resident, colonial at nesting time, but groups of nesters are never large. Most often seen in the southern dales, but there are two colonies near Bampton, in the north-east.

STARLING (*Sturnis vulgaris*)

Resident, common. Massive winter immigration from northern areas, both in Britain and on the Continent. Generally distributed at nesting time up to the tree limit, with the species using buildings and hollow trees as nesting sites. Quite large flocks of young birds may be seen in early summer, many of them frequenting the fell districts. Evening flights of starling flocks to communal roosts have been observed as early as July. Considerable roost at Leighton Moss.

GOLDEN ORIOLE (*Oriolus oriolus*)

The species nested in a Furness valley in 1958 and 1959.

JAY (*Garrulus glandarius*)
(CN - jay piet)

Locally common, mainly in southern woodlands, though it has been reported from Haweswater and near the outflow of Ullswater. Acorns provide a rich source of food for the jay in autumn and early winter.

MAGPIE (*Pica pica*)
(CN - piet)

Resident, common where there are no gamekeepers. Associated with both woodland and open country.

JACKDAW (*Corvus monedula*)
(CN - jack)

Many colonies in cliff faces, old buildings (such as barns and church towers). Individual pairs nest down almost every disused chimney. Quite large flocks in winter are often associated with other corvines.

ROOK (*Corvus frugilegus*)

Locally common. There is a large rookery in Serpentine Woods, Kendal, and 90-plus nests were noted in 1973. Rookeries tend to be on low ground, in areas of the richer farmland, but small rookeries have been established in fell districts. Rooks visit the high ground in early summer to feed on insects, notably the antler moth caterpillar. Such parties have been seen flying over the spurs of the fells from Kentmere to the head of Haweswater.

CARRION CROW (*Corvus corone*)
(CN—corbie, dope)

Resident, common, nesting up to 1,800 feet. Carrion crow numbers appear to remain stable, yet many hundreds of birds are slain each year by farmers and gamekeepers. There are quite large summertime roosts on crags, with over 100 birds at one roost in early June. Even larger roosts may be seen in winter.

RAVEN (*Corvus corax*)

Resident, mainly a crag-nester, with an estimated 60 pairs in Lakeland. In addition, there are many non-breeders or immature birds in the area. The Lakeland population, which has been stable for years, is possibly slowly rising. Nests are found mainly between 1,250 feet and 2,000 feet. Tree-nesting has been reported.

A BRIEF BIBLIOGRAPHY

Birds of Cumberland, Rev. H. A. Macpherson and William Duckworth (1886).

The Status and Distribution of Birds in Lancashire, K. G. Spencer (1973).

A Guide to the Birds and Flowers of the Silverdale-Arnside Area, including Leighton Moss RSPB reserve, John Wilson and Michael Thomas (1972).

The Birds of Lakeland, (1943), *Lakeland Ornithology* (1954) and *The Birds of the Lake Counties* (1962), the first two edited by E. Blezard, the last by R. Stokoe.

Cumbria magazine.